DISCARD

HOPE

Also by Bill Reynolds

HOPE

A SCHOOL, A TEAM, A DREAM

Bill Reynolds

ST. MARTIN'S PRESS
NEW YORK

HOPE. Copyright © 2016 by Bill Reynolds. All rights reserved. Printed in the United States of America. For information, address St. Martin's Press, 175 Fifth Avenue, New York, NY 10010.

www.stmartins.com

Designed by Omar Chapa

The Library of Congress Cataloging-in-Publication Data
is available upon request.

ISBN 978-1-250-08069-1 (hardcover)
ISBN 978-1-4668-9309-2 (e-book)

Our books may be purchased in bulk for promotional, educational, or business use. Please contact your local bookseller or the Macmillan Corporate and Premium Sales Department at (800) 221-7945, extension 5442, or by e-mail at MacmillanSpecialMarkets@macmillan.com.

First Edition: January 2016

10   9   8   7   6   5   4   3   2   1

R0444610794

To my sister, Polly Reynolds, whose courage and incredible spirit every day in the face of great physical difficulties is a daily inspiration

ACKNOWLEDGMENTS

My thanks go out to many people who helped me along the way. I am especially grateful to Dave Nyblom and his assistant coaches, Pedro Correia, Keith Moors, Jim Black, and Rob Whalen. They always made me feel welcome and have my enduring thanks. The Hope players could not have been better. They invited me into their world even in the most difficult of times, and if I got to know some better than others, they all have a piece of my heart.

David Vigliano has been my agent for almost thirty years now and always has been my advocate. He has my gratitude. I am fortunate to have once again worked with George Witte at St. Martin's Press. His insight, talent, and support made this a better book. He understood this project right from the beginning and no writer can ask for more. And also a public thank-you to Sara Thwaite at St. Martin's Press, whose patience, unfailing courtesy, and expertise helped to make this book a reality. Finally, I am once again indebted to Liz Abbott for her patience, support, and wise counsel.

HOPE

PROLOGUE

There is a Providence, Rhode Island, that most people never see.

It isn't the downtown that has been opened up by moving the paths of two rivers—an immense project that transformed a flood-prone aging infrastructure into a destination—where thousands pour into the city on soft summer nights to eat in fancy restaurants and watch gondola rides and see the rivers lit up in a ceremony called "WaterFire." It isn't Brown University, sitting up there on the top of College Hill, only a couple of blocks away from the statue of Roger Williams, the state's founder, overlooking the city like a benevolent father. It isn't the chic restaurants of Federal Hill, the spiritual home of the state's large Italian-American population.

This is inner-city Providence, at the intersection of South Providence and the West End neighborhood, a place commuters pass by as they hustle down I-95 to Cranston and Warwick and the rest of the southern suburbs. This is the Providence of sirens and gunshots in the night, of kids who live in fear, of gritty streets where there are too many drugs, too many gangs, too many guns, and too little hope that it's going to change anytime soon. This is the Providence that got left behind in the so-called Providence Renaissance in the '90s. A place you could spend your entire life in Rhode Island ignoring, a place where the American Dream has been under siege for a long time now.

I was there one cold December morning in 2011 to do a column for the *Providence Journal* on the death of former Hope High School basketball star Laurence Young, who had died unexpectedly while playing professional basketball in Brazil, the result of an infection after dental surgery. Basketball had taken Young far from the South Providence of his roots, a place where too many kids like him never make it out of the neighborhood. It had rescued him from a difficult home life, living with his aunt and helping her care for his grandfather, who was a double amputee. And it had given him a life that must have seemed unimaginable in 1999 when he graduated from Hope High School, just another inner-city kid with a future that seemingly stopped at next week.

The small storefront church on a narrow side street was jammed, and people kept coming up to the altar to talk about Young. Each one put a living face on the body that lay in the front of the church in an open casket, a gold basketball on his chest.

One of the speakers was Dave Nyblom, a burly white man in a dark suit who had coached Young at Hope High School about a decade earlier. He had always been more than just a coach to Young. He had been his advocate, believing that one day Young would be a college player when no one else saw that potential, bringing Young to summer camps and AAU tryouts, always touting him to college coaches. Young had never been a childhood phenom, someone anointed early by the basketball gods. He had been a skinny tenth-grader, and spent that season on the junior varsity team. And even after he had gone on to become a great player at Hope, making second-team All State in 1999, the high school cheers quickly faded into echoes. Young had nowhere to go, until finally Rider, a college in New Jersey, saw him at an AAU tournament in Providence and offered him a scholarship.

Nyblom had become a sort of surrogate father to Young, forever giving him rides home, past the drug dealers and the street people, past all the hangers-on who in their own ways were trying to steal Young's dream. When he heard on the phone that Young had died he started crying.

When it was his turn to speak Nyblom described what a good person Young had been, the emotion growing stronger in his voice with each passing sentence. In the back of the church was Nyblom's wife, his mother, and his two children. When he came to the end of his eulogy for Young, the tears were right there with the words.

"If there were two people I could see in Heaven it would be my father and Laurence," he said, his father having died twenty years earlier falling off a ladder while fixing a broken basketball hoop in Nyblom's hometown of South Kingstown, Rhode Island.

In many ways Young had not only been the prodigal son, he had also been the role model for many of the Hope players who had come after him. He was the one who had listened. He was the one who had bought in to Nyblom's vision for his players, the simple idea that if they did the right thing and worked hard they could escape the grim neighborhoods in which they were coming of age. He was the one who had said no to all the drug dealers. He was the one who had made it out, had overcome so many odds.

"He was like a son to me," Nyblom once said. "He always knew what to do."

Left unsaid was that there were so many others who hadn't known what to do.

And maybe now, there were more of those kids than ever.

If life in inner cities long has seemed to exact its own little pound of flesh, it's even harder now, as disparities in wealth divide neighborhoods. The crumbling economy has created a mélange of dysfunction, and communities are under siege. Providence is no exception. Gang violence. Shootings. Never-ending street crime. These are the almost daily news stories of horrors big and small, stories that amplify the sense that inner-city Providence is much more dangerous than it used to be, and that the kids who live in it are growing up in a cruel, dystopian landscape. Their world and its realities are rarely discussed in all the "race to the top" conversations, the national dialogue attempting to reform education, especially in the inner cities.

It's a world I have drifted in and out of through the decades, writing sports columns for the *Providence Journal*. One column was about Cedric Huntley, who had grown up on the streets of South Providence, one of the first black basketball players at a longtime Catholic school in Providence, and who worked for the Institute for the Study and Practice of Nonviolence.

"I wouldn't want to be a young person in this city," he had said. "It's so much worse than when I was a kid, and it wasn't good then."

He first got involved in working to reduce violence because he was going to too many funerals. Huntley had come to know how fragile it all is, how a kid's life can change in an instant. Joining a gang. Selling some drugs because everyone else is doing it. Engaging in foolish retribution for some perceived slight. Lives hinge on that one bad decision, all played out against a backdrop of poverty and broken families, the daily minefield so many of these kids walk through.

"If we don't help these kids, who is going to?" Huntley had asked.

Another piece had been about Roosevelt Benton, who on

an afternoon in 1995 was running the South Providence Boys &
Girls Club and was superintendent of programs at the state training school. He was one of the unsung heroes in Providence at the
time, a large black man with soft eyes that conveyed a certain
sadness.

"The biggest thing I've seen is the attitude of the kids,"
he said then. "The level of respect has changed dramatically. In
many cases, there's no respect. None whatsoever. The other
change is the lack of values and the desire for material things at
an earlier age.

"TV exerts a great influence on these kids," Benton continued. "It increases their desires. You've got to have the right
sneakers. The right sweatshirt. And, basically, we adults are
responsible for this. This is the society we've created, the society
these kids have grown up in. They see people respected for their
material things. Not for their value system. Not for their ethics.
Not for who they are as people. For their material things."

He paused then, and when he spoke again his voice was
softer, more resigned.

"It's much more difficult now for these kids than it was when
I grew up. We weren't exposed to crack. We weren't exposed
to guns. We weren't exposed to being able to make a hundred
dollars when you're twelve years old just by selling a couple of
vials on the corner. We weren't exposed to the advertising that
says if you don't wear two-hundred-dollar sneakers you're nobody."

That was thirteen years ago. It's even tougher now to be
young in this place.

In my columns, I usually focused on the kids who had gotten to college, the ones who had overcome so many of the odds,
whether it was through talent, good fortune, mentors in their
lives, or some other factor. Yes, their back stories were part of
their stories. But these were the kids who had made it, despite

the odds. They were the Laurence Youngs of the world. But what about the ones who probably were not going to make it in sports? What about the others?

This is Dave Nyblom's world. He's been coaching at Hope for twenty-four years, nineteen as the varsity basketball coach, driving up from southern Rhode Island every morning in a truck whose bed is often full of food because he long ago realized that some of his players don't get enough to eat. He's had a handful of ex-players die. He's had others end up in jail. He's heard for over two decades that inner-city kids are undisciplined, can't be disciplined. These are the stereotypes he's spent his entire adult life trying to refute.

And on this gray day in late November 2012, here in this old gym on the second floor of Hope High School, this massive red-brick building that first opened in 1936, he's about to try to refute these stereotypes once again.

CHAPTER ONE

"If you're not going to do it, just go home," Nyblom yelled as roughly thirty kids labored through push-ups on the old gym floor.

It was the first day of practice and Nyblom was wearing a dark blue short-sleeve shirt with "Hope" stitched over a pocket in white letters, baggy tan shorts, and white sneakers. Overhead, fifteen small blue-and-white banners hung from the ceiling, rectangular tributes to past glories. The walls of the gym were tan brick. There were five rows of dark blue bleachers on one side, and three on the other. A small American flag hung in one corner. Twelve large Palladium windows, six on each side, let in the winter light. One side of the gym looked out over a small courtyard in the middle of the school. The other side looked out to an athletic field in the back, and an affluent neighborhood across the street from the field, one of the oldest in Providence, dating back to the nineteenth century. The basketball court was old, worn by decades of kids running across it. The gym was showing its age, like some dowager who can't hide the years no matter what she does.

"That will get you a ticket right out of here," Nyblom said again in his big, loud voice as one kid threw up a ridiculous shot. "This isn't the playground."

But it sure seemed like it.

My last time in this gym had been in December 1961. I was a junior then, playing for a small suburban high school ten miles to the south. Hope was a city school that had won the state title the year before and had played in the New England Tournament in the old Boston Garden where the Celtics ruled, and on that long-ago winter night Hope beat us, one of only three losses the entire season. Even then, though, the gym was small and everything seemed old, and Kennedy was in the White House and no one had heard of the Beatles, never mind rap.

But if I hadn't been in the gym in over fifty years, I had driven by Hope countless times. I had played basketball at Brown University in the '60s, and Hope is only a few hundred yards away from the seventh oldest college in the country. Across Hope Street from the school is Moses Brown, a private school that's been in existence since 1819. Less than a mile away is the prestigious Rhode Island School of Design, which attracts students from all over the world. In front of that school is Benefit Street, the most historic street in Providence, which dates back to the seventeenth century and is now a historic landmark. Hope is on Providence's East Side, the oldest part of the city, an area rich in history that goes back to the beginnings of the country and the beginnings of Providence, an area now lined with million-dollar homes.

Hope was part of my history too, even if indirectly.

My father had played football for Hope back in the early '30s, when it was called Hope Street High School, an old red-brick school located across the street from where it is now; it had first opened in 1898. I have many friends who went to Hope back in the early '60s when it was a melting pot of sorts, full of kids who continued on to college and professional lives and remembered Hope fondly, seeing it as a pathway to success.

But I had seen it change, too. Through the years I had written a few columns on athletes from Hope. One was on a great runner, and we stood in a dirty locker room where too many locker doors were broken, hanging from their hinges. Another time, the football coach said his biggest problem was getting his kids to come to school five days in a row, his rule for who was eligible to play on Saturday. And just a few years ago, I had talked to a Hope football player who had lost one of his closest friends to gang violence, which has become an epidemic in inner-city Providence.

"In my age group, seventeen, eighteen years old, we fear for our lives," he had said quietly.

So what was going on here?

How did a school whose very name is the motto of Rhode Island become a symbol of everything wrong with American education in this new millenium—high dropout rates, absenteeism, violence, the materials outdated and the structure in disrepair, overcrowded with kids the country seems to have few answers for? More important, who are these kids that society seems to walk to the other side of the street to avoid? All these nonwhite, poor kids, the ones with their hoodies and baggy pants, who often fear for their lives?

Who are these kids?

It was the question the country was grappling with throughout 2012, after Trayvon Martin, a young black male in a hooded sweatshirt, was killed by a civilian in a gated community in Florida who believed he shouldn't have been there, must have been there to commit a crime.

So who are these kids?

And what do they dream?

In many ways they had become invisible to me, too. They were the kids you sometimes saw walking down Thayer Street, the hip commercial street full of Brown students, on their way to the nearby bus tunnel that went downtown. They were the ones you saw downtown on Kennedy Plaza in front of the gray stone City Hall where the buses from all over the city stop. They were the ones who played in the Rhode Island Interscholastic League that was traditionally dominated by Hendricken and La Salle, the two parochial school powerhouses. In so many ways, these kids from the public schools in Providence were out of sight, and out of mind, even in sports.

But who are they?

In December 2012 I decided to find out.

So there I was at the first day of practice, watching kids in their baggy shorts and different-colored sneakers, in their gym class T-shirts and their ragtag uniforms and their hopeful expressions. And at first glance it all looked like basketball chaos. One kid rocked a big Afro, as if he'd been transported from the '70s, complete with a red tattoo on his throat. One had a ponytail and the first initial of his first name tattooed on the back of one leg, and the first initial of his last name tattooed on the other. A couple of others styled their hair in cornrows. Two played with no shirts at all. They were all black kids, except for sophomore guard Angel Rivera, who had been born in Puerto Rico. This was supposed to be one of the best high school teams in Rhode Island?

Two starters were missing because they played on the football team, which had a playoff game scheduled for that night, and Wayne Clements, the starting point guard from last year, was recovering from knee surgery.

And where was Emmanuel Kargbo, whom everyone called Manny?

Manny was the best player at Hope, second-team All State a year ago in the *Providence Journal*. He was a six-foot-two senior, with wide shoulders and slim hips, and an expression that could turn from warm and happy to disconsolate in the blink of an eye. He had been born in war-torn Liberia, and remembers soldiers shooting during a soccer game between a Liberian team and one from Ghana in his native Monrovia. He came to Providence with his mother and two brothers in the summer before his freshman year, after living in Delaware since he was seven. But he still carried remnants of the Liberian English he had grown up speaking, to the point where he seemed to preface every sentence with "Yo, yo," as some sort of verbal warm-up.

Where was Manny?

"Something's going on with him," muttered Keith Moors, a six-foot-six light-skinned black man, a former prison guard, who has given countless hours of his time over the past six years as a volunteer assistant coach. "It's like he's fighting us."

Moors and Nyblom had first met at a Christmas party at a local sporting goods company six years ago. Moors had told Nyblom he was interested in getting into high school coaching. That was the beginning.

"Dave told me to come to practice, and I had never seen anything like it," he said. "Guys talking back. Guys getting thrown out of the gym. One took his shirt off and threw it on the floor. Another threw a trash can across the court. It was crazy. That whole season was crazy. Kids yelling when they got taken out of a game. Kids quitting. Others getting thrown off the team. It was like the Wild, Wild West and it sabotaged the whole season."

Not that Moors was a wide-eyed innocent. For years he was a guard at the Adult Correctional Institute in nearby Cranston, and he had his own dramatic back story. But this was a high school basketball team.

"It's always something," he continued. "Too many of these

kids have no structure in their lives. None. They're living with grandparents. Or an older sister or brother. You see where they come from. Where they live. It's scary. Ninety-eight percent are good kids. But there's nobody at home. No discipline. It's difficult. Because they don't want to open up, don't want to tell you what's really going on at home."

Moors looked out on the gym floor, lost in thought, as if seeing something only he could see.

"They all think they're going to the NBA," he said, resignedly. "Or at least going to a Division I college. It's unbelievable. You ask the seniors, 'What are you going to do next year?' They'll say college. Have you applied yet? No. Then you turn around the next year and they're back here in the gym asking for help. I should have listened, they say. Every year it's something. In '09 we had three kids get arrested for stealing some laptops and an iPod when we went across the street to play Moses Brown. The kids were lying to the cops, and the cops already had everything on tape. That sucked the life out of the whole season."

He paused.

"You see a little bit of everything here. It's always something."

He pointed at Nyblom, this big man with his shorts and sneakers and his cropped hair the color of sand, this man who had a visible presence, commanding the gym with a big voice and a natural whistle that seemed as loud as a real whistle.

"They think he's the enemy. He's not the enemy. He'd give his right arm for these kids. The problem is too many don't realize it until it's too late."

"WAKE UP!" yelled Nyblom as he watched the basketball sacrilege going on in front of him, a simple three-man weave being treated as if it were some mathematical equation.

"CATCH THE BALL. . . . BOUNCE PASS. . . . GO BEHIND HIM, ANGEL. . . . WAKE UP! If you can't pass and catch the ball, fellas, it's going to be a long season. How are we supposed to run a play when we can't even run a three-man weave without any defense? This is Basketball 101."

The drill continued, over and over, with similar results.

"TURNOVER CITY!" yelled Moors.

"Fellas, we can't keep doing this," said an exasperated Nyblom. "If we only have six guys who can do this then those are the six guys who will play, and everyone else will go home."

But they did keep doing it. It was a practice full of basketball atrocities.

And the next afternoon was more of the same, starting the minute practice began.

"LINE UP ON THE BASELINE!" yelled Nyblom.

Once again it looked like a ragtag group, more like a gym class than a high school basketball team.

"In order to play basketball you have to have your sneakers tied," he said, distinctly staring at one skinny kid who looked back at him, clueless.

"Yeah, you," Nyblom said.

Hope had lost in the state football playoffs the night before, so there were a handful of football players at practice, including two prospective starters. One was Delonce Wright, the best football player at Hope, a five-foot-ten kid who had run 4.37 in the forty-yard dash at the Boston College football camp, the kind of speed that gets everyone's attention in football.

There was something a little different about Wright. He seemed more socially poised than most of the other kids. Maybe that was because he had spent a year at St. Andrew's, a private school in suburban Barrington, before being thrown out after his freshman year for what had been called "bringing some product from his neighborhood to the campus." Or maybe it was because he had gone to the Paul Cuffee School in Providence as a kid, a school generally considered better than the

Providence public schools for so-called at-risk kids. You could have a conversation with Wright, which was more difficult to do with most of the other players.

The other football player was the dark-skinned Johnson Weah. He, too, had been born in Liberia. But his mother took him and his older brother to the Ivory Coast when he was just nine months old to escape the civil war that raged on for fourteen years. He only saw his father once, when his father made a short visit to the refugee camp where his family lived. He remembers him as "just a normal person who got caught up in the war." He spent the next eight years in a refugee camp, as his mother and older brother cut wood every day. He went to school, but it was basically just daycare. The only sport the refugee kids played was soccer, with a ball made out of old plastic bags.

"My mother worked with me on my ABCs and times tables," he said. "That was the highest education I had when I came to America."

He was ten years old, without any formal schooling, when he first came to Providence. He was put into the third grade.

"To be honest, I didn't feel like I was in my own body," he said of that first year in an American classroom, both older and bigger than anyone else around him, with a profound sense of displacement. He had arrived in a strange new world that no one had prepared him for. "I had a problem reading. I didn't mix in with the other kids. I felt left out."

Weah was six-foot-two, rock-solid, a player who didn't have many skills but was the very definition of tough and hardworking, the ideal teammate. He also knew how fortunate he was that his mother took him out of Liberia, for if he had stayed he would have been conscripted into the war, just another child soldier in a brutal war full of them.

"If I had stayed I would have been forced into it," he said softly.

He, too, carried his Liberian childhood in his speech.

"What language did you speak as a kid?" I asked him one day.

He looked at me as though he didn't understand the question.

"English."

So why can't I understand you, I wanted to say.

"Liberian English," he said, no doubt seeing my confusion.

"What's that?" I asked.

"You wouldn't understand," he said.

"Try me," I said.

He paused for a second, then looked at me.

"You, me, go to corner, yo?" he said in an almost singsong voice.

I would come to learn that Johnson Weah was very sensitive about his speech, to the point that he thought you were making fun of him if you had trouble understanding him and asked him to repeat himself. He was proud, almost regal in appearance, with ebony skin, and scars on his back that no one ever asked him about. But if Johnson didn't say much, there was no doubt he would try to run through a brick wall for his teammates, no questions asked.

The addition of Wright and Weah instantly made Hope better. Put them with Kargbo and junior Ben Vezele, the thin, long-armed left-handed forward, and there was no question Hope was an athletic high school team by Rhode Island standards.

The only problem?

The senior point guard was nowhere to be found.

I noticed him sitting by himself on the last row of the bleachers, as geographically isolated from the team as he appeared to be psychologically.

"I remember a kid puked in a bucket when I was a freshman

and I was nervous I was going to do it too," Wayne Clements said, almost to himself, as I sat down next to him.

He was thin, five-foot-ten or so, with cornrows and a boyish face. His entire persona screamed out too-cool, but every once in a while a smile would sneak across his face, like when he described how he broke his elbow.

"There was a big girl fight down on a field by Brown last spring and then three cops came and they were pepper-spraying everybody and I was running to get away and I jumped over a fence and fell on it."

This was said matter-of-factly, as if relating just another normal afternoon after school. He'd had surgery on his knee in August, after hurting it playing basketball over the summer, and more surgery in September after reinjuring it. And it wasn't better yet, much to the consternation of the coaches, who felt he wasn't exactly punishing himself in his rehab.

He had missed the state tournament last year because he and freshman Angel Rivera had been caught stealing two basketballs from the gym at East Providence High School during a game, an act that had been captured on videotape. The coaches believed Wayne's absence had prevented them from winning the state championship. Now he seemed to drift in and out of practice like a ghost, here one minute, gone the next, even though he said basketball was very important to him.

Certainly he had grown up with it. His father, Buster Clements, a one-time high school star in Providence, ran an inner-city rec center on Sacket Street in South Providence, so Wayne had started playing there as a young kid, along with several of his future Hope teammates. He'd wanted to go to private school in Rhode Island after the eighth grade, but his grades weren't good enough.

"Do you study now?"

"Not really," he said. "I was pretty good as a freshman, but then I got lazy."

He walked over to the treadmill by the door in the corner of the gym, got on it.

A few minutes later Nyblom walked over to him.

"You're on the treadmill?" he asked, stating the obvious.

"Yeah," Clements said.

"How long?"

"A long time."

"Five minutes," said Nyblom, walking away.

I had first met Nyblom about a decade earlier. He was a big man with a sandy-colored brush cut, one of those no-nonsense guys who seemed to have stepped off the pages of adolescent sports fiction. By chance we were on adjoining treadmills at the South County YMCA, about thirty-five miles south of Providence in South Kingstown, where he grew up and still lived. He said that every year he brought his team down for dinner at his house, and every year there were a couple of kids who had never eaten dinner at a table before, an image that's always stayed with me. One night, he said, the kids were going from his house to his mother's house a couple of hundred yards away in a field. It was dark and some of them had said they were afraid, and Nyblom had said, "How about I fire a few gunshots into the air so it will feel like home?"

The first game of the 2012–13 season was on December 7, a Friday night. It was Hope's only nonleague game and it was against Moses Brown, the private school across Hope Street. The school had been founded by Moses Brown, one half of the Brown brothers who had been instrumental in Providence's transformation from a small settlement at the base of College Hill into a city that sent ships all over the world. The Browns were one of the most powerful mercantile families in New England in the 1700s. Moses Brown had also been a central figure in the birth of the Industrial Revolution, the founder of what is considered to be one of the first factories in the country.

The root of the Brown family's vast wealth was their involvement in the triangular trade, between New England, Africa, and the West Indies. It was a rather sophisticated business for the eighteenth century. Molasses and sugar from the West Indies were distilled into rum, which was taken to Africa and traded for slaves, who, in turn, were brought to America. Both Providence and Newport, Rhode Island, thirty miles to the south down Narragansett Bay, were key cities in the American slave trade in the 1700s, and the Brown family had amassed amazing wealth. To this day the Brown family's legacy is deeply ingrained in Providence; Brown University is named for the family.

Moses Brown had become an abolitionist, eventually breaking away from his brother, John. After the death of his wife in 1773, he left the family business and became a Quaker, and spent the rest of his life speaking out against slavery, no insignificant thing given that his brother John was one of Rhode Island's leading slave traders. He started the school in 1787, and it moved to its present location on the East Side in 1819. It began as the New England Yearly Meeting Boarding School and was renamed nearly a century later in honor of Moses Brown. Now, 109 years after the school had been named for an abolitionist, its basketball team was playing against a nearly all black team in an America that no one back then, not even Moses Brown, could have begun to imagine.

The Hope team had been cut down to roughly fifteen kids, football player Corey Brinkman being the only white player, and they were sitting in the locker room near Nyblom's physical education office. It had blue lockers, a gray floor, and tan walls.

Outside its door was a large mural of five black football players in bright blue-and-yellow uniforms. Nyblom, wearing dark slacks and a white short-sleeve shirt with "Blue Wave" in small blue letters on the back, was passing out the home uniforms when Manny Kargbo walked in.

Manny had just been told he was not going to play against Moses Brown; he was being disciplined for what Nyblom called his poor attitude. He wasn't happy. Especially when he saw one of the young sophomore substitutes about to put on his white uniform top with "Blue Wave" on the front in blue lettering, and number 25 on the back.

"Are you all right with me wearing your number, Manny?" the kid, skinny and young looking, asked quietly.

"No," Kargbo said. "Take it off."

He was wearing jeans and a blue parka. "I guess the game tonight is not that important," he said to no one in particular, more as a defense mechanism than an attempt at bravado. Like many of the kids, Kargbo wore his emotions on his face, and when he wasn't happy he had a mournful look, like a pallbearer at a funeral.

He was not being punished for anything egregious, but it was Nyblom's way of sending him a public message that he didn't like the way Manny had been acting lately. His occasional tardiness. His moodiness. The sense that there were things going on in his life that he was not telling anyone about.

But Kargbo was not the only unhappy player heading into the first game. Angel Rivera, the sophomore point guard who was starting until Wayne Clements returned, had been caught cutting an English class and would spend the game on the bench. He wasn't happy either.

A few minutes later the team was upstairs in the Health Room, which also served as the team's study hall every afternoon before practice while the girls' team used the gym. It's around the corner from the gym and down a small flight of stairs, a big room with windows that looked out over the athletic fields in the back. There were various exhibits and messages on the walls, including a large one headlined, "Health Risks of Drug Use," with a list of assorted ills. The players sat in chairs at tables. Nyblom stood in the front of the room.

"Moses Brown only plays one Division I team and you are it," Nyblom said, "so you're going to get their best shot. So no personal highlight shows. Let's play together, and start to build something, okay?"

He hesitated a beat.

"How many of you have looked at the playbook we passed out?" he asked.

Four hands slowly went up.

"We're not prepared to play a game tonight, gentlemen," Nyblom continued. "We simply haven't had enough practice time. What we're looking for tonight is great effort. If you are hustling, diving on the floor, doing what you can do to help us win, that's what we're looking for."

The starting lineup was junior Ben Vezele; five-foot-ten senior Dennis Wilson, a valuable piece of the Hope team that had lost in the state finals at the University of Rhode Island last March; junior Marquis Young, the nephew of Laurence Young; junior big man Quenton Marrow; and sophomore Eli Lewis, who had recently moved to Providence from Bridgeport, Connecticut. Only Vezele figured to start next week when the league season began.

The lineup didn't make much difference.

Hope was expected to beat Moses Brown, regardless of the fact that they hadn't practiced and Kargbo wasn't going to play. Moses Brown started four white kids and Hope was simply too athletic for them, their smothering defense the key to the game. Not that a tape of the game was ever going to be sent to the

Basketball of Fame. Neither team could do much offensively. Nobody made many perimeter shots. The game was sloppy, played before a couple hundred people in the old second-floor gym with wire over the windows, what the gym in the movie *Hoosiers* would have looked like if it had been set in an inner-city neighborhood in the '50s and not in rural Indiana. Hope won 58-41, and the Moses Brown parents, about a dozen who had sat together near the door, seemed to fast break out of the gym as soon as the game ended, as if their field trip to the inner city had just ended and they couldn't wait to get out.

"I think that's your 968th career win," Moors said to Nyblom as they walked off the court together.

Nyblom laughed.

"One down, twenty-three more to go," he said.

They were all back in the Hope gym the next morning for a scrimmage against a team from Ledyard, Connecticut, the town near the southern Rhode Island border where Foxwoods Casino, one of the biggest in the country, is located. Nyblom likes to schedule either extra games or scrimmages on Saturdays, always against good opponents who will test his team, games that don't count on the record. It was a raw, gray day in early December, the promise of winter in the air, and it was cold in the gym, as if the week's allotment of heat had been used up the night before.

Before Norwich arrived the atmosphere was low key. Three boxes of doughnuts sat on the scorer's table. Nyblom, Moors, and the two other volunteer coaches, Rob Whalen and Jim Black, were going through the box scores of Friday night's high school games in the *Providence Journal*, as if checking in on old friends. Rhode Island is small, and the Rhode Island Interscholastic League is smaller, a basketball village where everyone listens to the same drumbeats.

Jeremy Rivera, who said he's Angel's cousin, was telling

anyone who would listen that he doesn't want to go to college, wants to go right to the NBA instead. Whalen, thin, with short dark hair, smiled ruefully and rolled his eyes.

"He quit last year," said Whalen, pointing at Jeremy Rivera, "then he became our biggest cheerleader."

Five kids who used to play for Hope were in the gym. Moors calls them "alumni."

"We probably had ten of them here last night," he said. "You ask them what they're doing and they say nothing. They don't go to school. They don't have a job. There's often a couple of them here every day because they really have nowhere else to go. Then they say they should have listened to us. It's sad. That will be Wayne Clements next year, mark my words."

He looked out on the court.

"These kids don't get it. They don't go to school. They miss practice. And when you call them on it they pout. Dave's always getting calls from colleges: 'You got anybody?' He will find them a place to play, but they have to do their part too."

All the players were in the gym—except Manny Kargbo.

"I don't get it," Moors continued. "He's throwing his senior year away. Like last night, saying it must not be an important game."

A few minutes later Nyblom walked in.

"Where's Manny?" Rob Whalen asked.

"He's on the bus."

"Did he call you?"

"I called him," Nyblom said.

Finally Manny walked into the gym.

"ALL WORLD!" Moors yelled out, a big smile on his face.

"The only problem," Rob Whalen said quietly, "is he believes it."

The team from Connecticut began warming up at one end of the gym, while Nyblom talked to his team at the other.

"We are here to execute plays, gentlemen," he said quietly.
"Not to laugh and joke. Not to fool around. But to run plays.
Because last night we couldn't run any. And I guarantee you that
when we start running plays in games you will not know them.
It's real simple, gentlemen. You've got to get serious and you have
to figure out what we're trying to do."

Once again, there were three alumni in the gym. One was
Malieke Young, a small, wiry black kid with an orange streak
running through his tight Afro. He is Laurence Young's nephew,
and his younger brother, Marquis, was a junior on the team fighting for playing time. Their mother, whom Nyblom taught when
she had been a student at Hope, was sixteen years old when she
gave birth to Malieke. His father was in jail. Last year Malieke
started on the Hope team that lost in the state finals in the Ryan
Center at the University of Rhode Island; he was a good player
who could make shots. Then the season ended, and Malieke
Young became an unfortunate statistic, another young African-
American kid who was not in college and didn't have a job, no
big surprise in a state with the second highest unemployment rate
in the country. When his senior year ended no schools came calling. So now he was in limbo, hoping he might get an opportunity next year to go off to junior college and chase the basketball
dream. He was killing time, hoping Nyblom could hook him
up somewhere.

Another one of the so-called alumni was also in the gym.

But Roland Hannah was different, and not just because he
went on to play big-time college basketball at the University of
New Mexico after two years at a Nebraska junior college. Nor
was he different because he was six-foot-six, with a shaved head
and the kind of strong body that easily adjusted to the college
game. He was different because he was one of the kids who listened, who was able to transcend this old gym in this old school.

"I never had a father," he said as he watched Hope warm

up. "There were three kids and I was the youngest. My mother was everything. We came to America when I was five years old from Liberia. We landed in Newark, New Jersey. I had never seen such big buildings and I was scared. But I wanted to see America, too."

He stopped and stared out at the court, as if the past were like a newsreel running through his head.

"African families are very strict. Much stricter than American families. I couldn't say the word 'stupid' in front of my mother, and when I was a kid I had to be home when the streetlights came on."

He had gone to grammar school and the Roger Williams Middle School in South Providence, the inner city for over a half century now. And he always took school seriously, because his mother, who worked as a nurse's aide, *made* him take school seriously, to the point that if he didn't she wasn't going to let him play basketball. In the ninth grade he went to Hope.

By then, Hannah knew he wanted to play college basketball. But he couldn't make the minimum eligibility score on the SAT test, so he wasn't able to receive a scholarship. On a test where the maximum score was 1600, and you got 400 points for signing your name, he got a 496. He was bitter about it. He had never been a troublemaker in school, always had done his homework. He had also always done what the teachers asked, because he wanted to please his mother, who he felt had sacrificed so much for him. Yet when it came time to take the SATs he was woefully deficient. He was a two-time All State player, but for the longest time it seemed as if he would never step foot on a college campus. He felt betrayed, and believed that the educational system had failed him.

"The problem is a lot of teachers lump us all together," he said. "The kids who don't care, and the kids who do. I wasn't prepared for the SAT test in anyway. It was full of things I had never seen before. I saw all those big words in the verbal part and it was like I was standing in a big crowd, but I was all alone. You're all alone and you're lost."

He'd been a senior at Hope in the spring of 1995. That same spring he'd been a part of a group of Hope students who had marched on Providence's City Hall to protest the ouster of the school's principal after one year, a man whose first year at Hope had become a firestorm of controversy. Hope found itself all over the local news, complete with charges of racism and backlash, a microcosm of many of the racial tensions that were dividing society.

Hannah's story, however, had a successful ending. He got help from a man named Bob Dyer, whose son had played against Hannah in high school. Dyer learned of his predicament and volunteered to tutor him. So they began meeting every morning before school on Thayer Street, just down the street from Hope in the virtual heart of Brown University, to prep for the test; Dyer drove into South Providence every morning to pick him up. And on his fourth attempt Hannah met the minimum score. After two years at McCook Junior College in Nebraska, where he became so focused that he would often sleep in the gym, he won a scholarship to New Mexico.

Now he's a guard at the Training School in Cranston, where he deals with inner-city kids who walked the same streets of his childhood.

"They all want it now," he said, looking out at the court, as if thinking of all those early mornings with Bob Dyer studying for the SATs, all those early mornings that, in retrospect, meant everything. "They don't want to wait for it. And they don't want to work for it. They want it now."

What is left unsaid is that they don't want it the way he once wanted it.

By the time the scrimmage started there were about fifty

people watching. Ledyard was an all-black team, and right from the outset Hope was in trouble, quickly down 10-0. Unlike the night before, where their athleticism dominated Moses Brown, now all their flaws were instantly exposed. The lack of strong point guard play. The inability to run any real offense. The lack of practice time. The fact that any kind of defensive pressure instantly made them come unglued. The sense that they played like a pickup team that had first met about ten minutes before the scrimmage.

"PASS THE BALL!" screamed Nyblom. "ANGEL, MAKE HIM GO LEFT. HE WANTS TO GO RIGHT. MAKE HIM GO LEFT. . . . CAN'T WE RUN A PLAY?"

This was a team ready for its league season to start in just three days?

CHAPTER TWO

"Johnson's miserable today," Moors said as I walked into practice two days later. "Someone's always miserable. Today it's Johnson. It's been Manny. But Manny's happy today."

Kids brought their personal lives into the gym every afternoon, right there with their sneakers. What was going on at home? Who was hassling them in school? Whose girlfriend was saying she might be pregnant? Who had to spend time in "Credit Recovery," an after-school program designed to resurrect failing grades? These kids so often were negotiating minefields in one form or another, and the subtexts meant that no two practices ever seemed the same.

It was another gray, rainy day, winter in New England in early December. And once again, Nyblom was working on the half-court offense, as if it had become his personal Great White Whale.

There were reasons for the difficulty, of course, the main one being that inner-city kids traditionally struggle against zones, not just here in Providence, but everywhere. Playground

basketball is street ball, always man-to-man, always confronta-
tional, a game in which how someone takes the ball to the hoop
is the definition of machismo. It's a basketball version of performance art, the more flair the better, basketball as theater. This is
not only how city kids come of age in the game, it's what they
admire. The great handle. The ability to shake and bake. The
ability to take someone off the dribble, break them down, if you
will, both physically and psychologically. This is the personification of playground basketball, in which style is not only king,
it's everything.

It's also the way most AAU games are played. AAU games,
the off-season matchups that nearly every kid serious about
basketball in the country plays, tend to be very similar, style-
wise: press on defense and play up-tempo on offense, glorified
street ball with a patina of structure. Most of the Hope players
were on an AAU team, three playing on Team Providence,
coached by Jim Black. And since there hasn't been any middle
school basketball in Providence in roughly two decades, kids
often learn basketball in an unstructured way. Is it any wonder
that so many inner-city kids don't like to play against zones, see
them as almost unfair and certainly not real basketball? Is it any
wonder that virtually every suburban high school team in America plays city schools zone?

"PASS THE BALL!" yelled Nyblom after another unsuc-
cessful attempt to dribble through a zone resulted in a turnover.
"WHY IS IT SO DIFFICULT?"

A question that seemed as unanswerable as Is there a God?

"Are we on offense or defense?" asked a burly kid.

"Figure it out, Devante," Nyblom said, shaking his head.

Hope will play the next day at Hendricken, always one of
the state powers, and Nyblom knew his team was nowhere near
ready. He also knew that this is just the way it is, a season that
begins too quickly, so there's never enough practice time. Last

year Hope had begun the season 2-7 for many of the same reasons. To Nyblom, though, it was always the same story, each season starting out like a large puzzle whose pieces are scattered all over the floor.

"Do you realize that no one has scored a basket yet?" he said, an edge in his voice. "Ben, I know you don't want to be short with your shot, but what are you trying to do, break the backboard with that line drive?"

Ben Vezele never said much, rarely showed any emotion. He didn't this time, either. He was a junior, a good student on a team with very few of them, seeming to glide through life a little more easily than most of the others did. This time, though, you could tell he didn't like Nyblom yelling at him. He looked straight ahead and not at Nyblom.

On and on it went, these little half-court scrums, full of missed shots and turnovers, with Nyblom's booming voice as the soundtrack: "Ben, don't get pissed, I'm trying to make you a better player. . . . Smart decisions, Angel. . . . Does anyone know what we're trying to run, or is this just a complete waste of time? . . . Devante, are you out of shape, or just plain lazy?"

Wayne Clements was shooting around at the other end of the gym, limping while getting his own rebounds.

"WAKE UP," yelled Nyblom. "We have a league game tomorrow. WAKE UP."

"Anyone here actually play last year?" Moors asked loudly.

"Doesn't look like it," Nyblom said.

A few minutes later Moors walked over and sat down in the front row of the blue bleachers, a disgusted look on his face.

"Another shitty-ass practice," he said, almost to himself. "It's starting to look like last year when we started out 2-7 and we got so disgusted one day that we put the clock on and made them just start running in a circle, over and over. No practice. Just run. Eventually we just told them to go home. That's how bad it was.

Then we went to play at North Kingstown in mid-January, had a great game, and that turned our whole season around."

Nyblom and Moors were sitting late Tuesday afternoon in the phys. ed office, a small, cluttered, L-shaped room dominated by a white refrigerator, a battered desk, and a couple of old chairs. There were eleven blue lockers and a floor that had started out red and had worn through the decades to a dull tan. The walls were tan brick, and boxes were stacked in a corner. There was a small bathroom and a shower off to one side, but the entrance-way was so cramped that if two kids came through the door there'd be a traffic jam, and if three adults were in the room at the same time it would seem like an old bus station with too many people in it.

On the wall was a clock that said 6:32.

It was about the fourth time I'd seen it say 6:32.

"How long has the clock been broken?" I asked.

Nyblom looked up at it with a bemused smile on his face.

"I've been here twenty-four years," he said.

He was twenty-six when he first came to Hope, and at the time it might have seemed like a strange fit, a white man coaching basketball in an almost completely nonwhite school, but he had never seen it that way, even if others did. To him there wasn't a black way to play basketball and there wasn't a white way; there was just the right way. This was the language of the game he always was trying to stress, that beneath all the differing styles of the game, all the differing theories, there were enduring themes that ran through it forever: be unselfish, play together, be a good teammate. All the basic truths that were as applicable to the Boston Celtics as they were to Hope High School.

He had grown up in a small town on the southern Rhode Island coast. It's also the home of the University of Rhode Island, a town that had always had both an African-American community and a Native American one, so he had played in high school with people of color, had always felt comfortable with them. He had been a glue guy as a high school player, one of those tough kids who didn't score many points, but always guarded the other team's best player, always played hard, and would have run through the gym wall if he thought it was going to help his team win. It was a style that won him a chance to play college basketball, at Norwich, a small school in Vermont. And it was a style he'd carried with him as a coach: play hard, be a good teammate, do the right thing. It's the message he'd been giving his players at Hope for nearly a quarter of a century, through all the years and all the seasons, all the games and all the kids.

When he first began coaching at Hope as a volunteer assistant in 1989 his friends began calling him "the White Shadow," a reference to the popular television show that had run in the '70s. The show was about a white coach, played by Ken Howard—who in real life had played college basketball at Amherst—leading an inner-city high school team in Los Angeles. To Nyblom, sports were the great common denominator, and from the beginning he had felt comfortable, even though there had been people in the local minority community publicly wondering why a white guy was coaching Hope. In Nyblom's sixth year at Hope, the longtime head coach had retired in the fall, and Nyblom had taken over the team as the acting head coach, without any pay, while his real job was being a physical education teacher at the school. Nor had he been paid in his five years as an assistant coach, essentially volunteering his time. In fact, it wasn't until a story in the sports section of the *Providence Journal* made this public, saying, "Hey Hope, Do the right thing: Hire Dave Nyblom," that he officially got the job.

But he had seen attitudes about race change as both Providence and Hope had changed, both now being roughly 60 percent

Hispanic. When he had first started coaching there it had been overwhelmingly African American.

"There are Asian kids in Hope that won't try and play for us because they say basketball is a black sport," he said, shaking his head at the apparent incongruity of it all, "and we have blacks who will not play baseball because they say it's a Hispanic game."

And he had seen basketball change in Providence too, no question about it. The rise of AAU culture, with its emphasis on "me." The increased cherry-picking by the private schools of many of the better black players. The presence of social media, where a player's performance was instantly critiqued, there for everyone to see, putting pressure on both players and coaches, making everything public. The widespread belief that basketball was the city game, the ticket to the good life. The belief that basketball was a black game, to the point that if you were black and not particularly good at it you were almost defying conventional wisdom, complete with the shame and embarrassment that came with failing to live up to that expectation.

These were some of the pressures that weighed on his players' shoulders, some lighter than others, but there nonetheless. But other things had changed in his time at Hope; life had become more hard-edged. On this team there was not one player on the roster who didn't have to take two buses every morning to get to Hope, even though the Mount Hope neighborhood, which included the mostly nonwhite Camp Street area, bordered Hope to the north.

Neighborhood school?

Not for the basketball players.

Nor for any other kid in Providence, for that matter, with countless kids taking two buses to get to school every morning and two more to get back at night.

That situation had started about five or six years ago, the result of a couple of factors. One was that Hope competed in

Division IV in football, the smallest division in the smallest state in the country, so many Camp Street kids who played football as well as basketball usually looked elsewhere for school, and in a city where there were no neighborhood high schools anymore, that was easy to do. Another reason was that the parochial schools in the state welcomed more minority athletes than they'd ever admitted before. So Hope's roster was full of kids from all over Providence, and Nyblom was constantly handing out bus tickets for the city buses, paid by the School Department.

Now they were waiting for the bus that would take them to Hendricken. There's little question that Hendricken, a Catholic school in Warwick, about ten miles south, is the gold standard of the Interscholastic League. The Hawks have won over a hundred state titles since the school began in 1959, and have sent Rocco Baldelli off to Major League Baseball, Will Blackmon to the NFL, Joe Mazzulla to star for West Virginia in the NCAA basketball tournament, and the Baron brothers to the University of Rhode Island, where they both went on to star for their father, Jim Baron. The Hendricken team is coached by Jamal Gomes, a light-skinned black man who has continued the long success of basketball at the school, winning five state championships.

In many ways Hendricken is the anti-Hope, a private all-boys school where the kids wear ties every day and where nearly all the seniors go off to college. It's a school whose radio ads promote both its academic heritage and its athletic one. It's not Moses Brown, with its look of old money and its patrician roots that go back centuries, but it's not the public schools, either. It promotes its differences: it's more structured, it's more focused, it has more of a sense of place; it's a school whose students are reminded of the school's tradition—and are now part of that tradition. In so many ways this is the opposite message that emanates from many public schools, especially inner-city ones, where history is just another class no one likes and "tradition" is just another word that has all but lost its meaning.

Rhode Island is one of the few states in the country where the parochial schools compete for the same state title as the public schools, courtesy of the state's size and athletic history. And when it's questioned, it's almost always answered in the same way: that's Rhode Island, as if that somehow explains everything.

"We haven't beaten Hendricken in six years," muttered Moors.

Hendricken would be a homecoming for Jim Black, a big guy who once played there. In his early twenties, with short-cropped dark hair, Black wanted to be a coach to the point that he stocked shelves at Stop & Shop overnight so he would have time to coach in the afternoons. He had gotten into coaching with an AAU team called Team Providence, where he had coached Ben Vezele and Wayne Clements, in addition to some other inner-city kids who played in the Interscholastic League. It had been an eye-opener, for some of the issues he dealt with were issues he had never seen during his time at Hendricken. He saw the fragile family situations. He saw the kids whose fathers were in and out of their lives, and since he too had been raised in a single-parent home he understood the pressures on them. He was up for a couple of jayvee jobs around the state, but they had fallen through, and before last season Nyblom had talked him into volunteering at Hope.

But even with his experience with Team Providence he wasn't prepared for the realities of Hope.

"If Nyblom didn't bring in the pork sandwiches and always be handing out cereal bars and fruit juice some of these kids wouldn't eat," Black said. "That's what people don't see. But when I first got here Pedro Correia [another volunteer coach] told me that it's not always about winning. At the time I didn't know what he was talking about. What do you mean it isn't about winning? I thought it always was about winning. It took me a while for me to see it, but I finally got it."

The yellow school bus was in the parking lot behind the school and it was full, two to a seat, the jayvee team also on the bus. It was nearly dark when the bus pulled out of the parking lot, took a left onto Olney Street, and started going down the hill toward downtown. In many ways Olney Street is the unofficial demarcation line between the rest of the East Side and the small black neighborhood that once was called Camp Street, named after the main street that cuts through it, and now is called Mount Hope. The neighborhood has been there since the late nineteenth century when real estate speculators began to build more housing to accommodate the city's growing population of factory workers, many of whom were working on nearby North Main Street, the site of many of the city's first factories. Streetcars had come to North Main Street in 1875. Eleven years later they came to Camp Street, which led to more housing being built. Many of these new residents were African American, and for decades the area was diverse in ways that much of the city was not. By the 1960s much of the Camp Street neighborhood was black, with Hope Street being the unofficial dividing line. African Americans lived west of Hope Street and down the hill to North Main Street. They did not live east of it, the beginning of Providence's wealthiest section.

In the '50's, at the foot of North Main Street, bordering downtown, there had been a small black section called Randall Square that had contained several black nightclubs. One was called the Celebrity Club, believed to have been one of the first interracial clubs in New England. In its heyday in the '50s some of the top jazz and rhythm-and-blues acts played the Celebrity Club, people like Louis Armstrong and Billie Holiday, Duke Ellington and Ella Fitzgerald. The club had closed in the early '60s, a victim of urban renewal, and now it's just history and old people's memories, music blowing in the wind. University Heights, an apartment complex that was built in the '60s, irrevocably changed the Camp Street neighborhood, and a shopping plaza at the foot of North Main Street did too. Still, Camp Street remains, a sliver of the inner city on Providence's East Side. It's long been an uneasy alliance. "White flight" from the Camp Street area started fifty year ago. Richard Rose, a black lawyer and community leader, says, not completely hyperbolically, "If too many kids from Camp Street were spending a lot of time east of Hope Street and down on Blackstone Boulevard where the real rich people in Providence are, there would be SWAT teams in here."

The bus went north on North Main Street and quickly exited onto I-95 heading south. The highway bisects Providence, separating downtown from Federal Hill and other parts of the city to the west. The lighted State House was to the left, as were the lights of downtown. The bus was quiet as it moved along with the heavy traffic, past lighted buildings and the new Providence Place Mall and the Dunkin' Donuts Center. Soon Rhode Island Hospital was on the right, and then a few miles later south on I-95 the state prison was visible. Hendricken is in Warwick, near the state airport. The entire ride took no more than twenty minutes, and that was in drive-time traffic. But it was out of the city, already a different world than the one the Hope kids lived in.

"Do you know where you are?" I asked Wayne Clements.

"Not really," he shrugged.

No surprise.

Hendricken is everything Hope is not.

The location is the first clue. Hendricken is a suburban school surrounded by parking lots in the front and spacious athletic fields off to the right. There is a well-groomed football field, home base for teams that always are among the Interscholastic

League's best in football, baseball, lacrosse, and track, in addition to basketball.

Inside, green-and-gold championship banners adorn the gym walls. Championship banners in basketball, football, baseball, hockey, track, golf. It's a tradition that goes back more than fifty years now at this all-male school where boys dress up for school every day and are expected to attend four-year colleges.

At halftime of the jayvee game the Hope players walked down a couple of clean, well-lighted corridors, past a "Memoriam" wall display of graduates killed in war, and into a classroom that had moveable desks and a picture of William Shakespeare on the white wall, along with the American flag. A bust of Jesus Christ was mounted on the wall over the desk, a visible reminder that Hendricken is a Catholic school.

The players began changing into their dark blue uniforms with their gold trim and "Hope" in big white letters. Nyblom was taping the ankles of Delonce Wright and Johnson Weah, the two football players, who sat on two green desks.

A few minutes later Wright got up and began walking around the room with his sneakers untied.

"Yo, Delonce," said Nyblom. "You going to play like that?"

"They don't teach us how to tie our shoes in school," he said, as everyone laughed.

"Okay, gentleman, listen up," Nyblom said. "They have more players than we have. They have practiced more than we have. We are working on playing hard. They don't want to run, and we want to get up and down. But it's our physical and mental toughness that will give us a chance."

He paused for a second.

"Last year when you bought in we got to the state finals," he said. "Let's not take that long to buy in this year. All right, bring it in."

They met in the front of the room, all huddled around Nyblom, their arms raised, their hands clasped together.

"ONE, TWO THREE, HOPE!" they shouted.

It was a different Hendricken team in several ways. For one, they didn't have the great player, the kind Hendricken has so often featured through the years. Ricky Ledo, for example, was an inner-city Providence kid who in just a few months would be selected in the 2013 NBA Draft, going in the second round to the Dallas Mavericks, having never played a minute of college basketball. Ledo had spent his freshman and sophomore year at Hendricken, playing on a state championship team.

"They look like us," quipped Moors.

Hendricken was coached by Jamal Gomes, who has a black father, a white mother, and his own emotional journey because of his mixed-race childhood. He had grown up in a white section of Cranston, which borders Providence to the south, but he had white cousins, and he had black cousins, and he looked white, and what kind of a name was "Jamal Gomes," anyway? Throughout his childhood he was always trying to figure out which side of his family he should identify with, and when he first went to Hendricken as a student he didn't like it. His mother essentially said "Deal with it."

There was also a certain irony to Gomes being the Hendricken coach, the perception being that Hendricken is the white-bread school that is so hugely successful in Rhode Island schoolboy sports. It's always been more complicated than that, but there's little question that Gomes didn't fit the stereotype. He was only the third basketball coach in the school's history, and in many ways it was a fluke when he got the job. He was twenty-six and had been the new assistant when the head coach abruptly resigned two weeks into the season in December 2000.

"Everything landed in my lap," he said, "and I knew I wasn't ready for it. It was crazy."

Then he went out and lost something like six out of his first seven games and wondered what he had gotten himself into. But slowly the team improved, ended the year losing in the state finals, and Gomes told himself that maybe he could do this after all.

It was now twelve years later. But he had learned that even though the state titles are wonderful, the essence of coaching is taking a group of kids and trying to get them to reach their potential, whatever that might be. And he'd learned that the real legacy is what you leave behind. It was the lesson he was always trying to teach his players, that the tradition is not just the banners on the walls, but the worth ethic and commitment, a legacy for others to follow. And the last thing he had learned, maybe the most important of all, was that it no longer mattered what race he is, black, white, or something in between. He'd learned that he's a father, a husband, a teacher, a coach. The rest just gets in the way.

Hendricken had easily beaten Hope both in the Providence summer league and in the fall league.

"That was the game Manny showed up in the second half—we were down twenty—then he got called for his fifth foul and was disqualified," Moors said, "but he wouldn't get off the court and we had to forfeit. Manny being Manny."

It was a Rhode Island high school gym right out of Central Casting, might hold a thousand people if you could shoehorn them all in. On this night there were a couple hundred, and from the beginning the game was awful, another gym class masquerading as a high school basketball game. After five and a half minutes Hope was down 2-0, and Nyblom called time out.

"Do you think we can score this half?" he said, his face flushed, as the team huddled around. "Our defense is good. Our intensity is good. Just slow down on offense, fellas, and run our stuff and get something good every trip down the floor."

He turned to a couple of guys he knew sitting behind the Hope bench and rolled his eyes.

"Welcome to Division I basketball in 1942," Moors said.

At halftime they were down 16-14 and the second half was more of the same, a dogfight to the end. The game seesawed back and forth, neither team scoring easily, Hope down one with 1:19 to play. Then Manny Kargbo scored on a drive with under a minute left, and Hope led by one, the pace frenetic, until Hendricken scored at the buzzer and escaped with the win.

"You are upset that you lost," said Nyblom in a soft voice back in the classroom. "You should be. You should be. You played your hearts out and it came down to the last shot. Don't worry. It will come. It's only one game. Last year we started out 2-7. This year we're going to turn it around quicker."

He paused for a few seconds, in the classroom with the bust of Jesus on the wall, as if he had already moved on from the game. "A kid who once played for me died three years ago today. So this is a difficult time for me."

He stopped, took a breath, and when he spoke again he was almost talking to himself as well as the players who sat in the moveable desks in the well-lit room and looked back at him.

"So please, please, please, take the time to enjoy this. Have some fun."

He turned to Jeremy Rivera, a small Hispanic kid with his dark hair pulled back in a ponytail. Rivera was slouched in his seat, a dejected look on his face.

"Jeremy, I know you're upset that you didn't play. Come back tomorrow and take this disappointment and turn it into something positive.

"For the rest of you, defensively you were very, very good. Let the loss hurt. Absolutely let it hurt. But let's be ready to go tomorrow."

Minutes later the team began putting their clothes on

over their uniforms, getting ready to leave. No one took a shower. Then again, no one ever took a shower. Practice would end and the players would put their clothes on over their practice gear and walk out of the gym. Tonight was the same routine.

"One more thing, gentlemen," Nyblom said. He pointed to a six-foot-four junior center named Quenton Marrow, a thin black kid who wore glasses and always seemed to play with enthusiasm, whether it was going through the most tedious of drills or running laps around the gym with his long strides, always coming in first because he ran the hardest. "You didn't play one minute tonight. But you were cheering on your teammates all night long. You were always enthusiastic and engaged. You were in every huddle, getting guys pumped up. You were tremendous."

The plan was to stay off I-95 on the way back to Providence, to go from Warwick into Cranston and then into the section of the city known as South Providence, or South Side, as it's now often called. Once it had been the home of innumerable Irish immigrants, who had come there in the first half of the nineteenth century and the first half of the twentieth century due to the potato famine in Ireland. That always had been the unofficial story of the melting pot that was Providence back then, scores of new immigrants to work in all the red-brick factories and innumerable jewelry shops that had come to define the city. As far back as the nineteenth century Providence was home to several of the largest manufacturing plants in the country, mostly owned by men who built big stately houses on the city's East Side. The plants attracted immigrants from Italy, England, and other European countries, in addition to Ireland, and also from Cape Verde and Canada. From 1865 to 1900 the city's population went from nearly 55,000 to 175,000, and by 1910 seven out of every ten people in the Rhode Island census were of either foreign birth or foreign parentage. Providence was the second biggest city in New England, an hour south of Boston. But it had always been its own world, as if Rhode Island were a city-state, with everything revolving around Providence, the only real city in the nation's smallest state.

The textile industry was already in trouble in Rhode Island by the time of the Depression in the early 1930s, and in many ways Providence's golden era was over. With the exception of the East Side, much of the city was blue collar and working class, and it had a reputation for being the mob capital of New England; the region's reputed crime boss Raymond Patriarca ran things from his storefront vending machine company on Atwells Avenue on Federal Hill, the home to the city's large Italian population. This was the Providence of urban legend a half century ago, a place of wooden three-deckers and men who went off to work carrying lunch pails, people whose dreams were to get their families out to the suburbs. It also was a heavily Democratic city, and the perception was that to get a city job you had to know somebody.

The so-called Providence Renaissance started in the 1990s. It was spearheaded by Vincent A. "Buddy" Cianci, the city's first mayor of Italian heritage, and from the moment he took office he was like a strong wind blowing down a dusty corridor. It was said that he would go to the opening of an envelope. Cianci was everywhere, out every night, to see and be seen. He would sit in the back of a town car and navigate his city, forever touting it, believing in it when so many others no longer did. He was charismatic, he was controversial, and in many ways he was larger than life. Cianci was convicted of "running a criminal enterprise" in 1996 and went to prison for five years, only to return and host a popular daily radio show. Whatever his flaws, many believed he left behind a better Providence, a city that had come to believe in itself again. A new shopping mall called Providence

Place stretched from downtown to the State House to the north. Waterplace Park, across the street from the mall, also took advantage of the Providence River, opening it up, making it an important part of downtown in ways it had never been before. The development had given the city a boost, best symbolized by an artist's idea to create "WaterFire," periodic nights when parts of the river were lit up and people would flock into downtown in an homage to the river and a civic celebration, a symbol of the city trying to reinvent itself for a new century.

The yellow school bus went through the residential neighborhoods of Pawtuxet Village and Edgewood, heading north on Broad Street toward the Providence line, just a couple of miles away. Shortly into Providence the bus stopped and two jayvee kids got out. Another block or two and the bus stopped again, and a couple more kids got out, as if the bus had turned into a city bus.

"Just say when," Nyblom yelled to the darkened back of the bus.

For although the bus was headed into Kennedy Plaza across from City Hall, the big switch point for buses where many of the kids would get off and take a city bus home, many of the players lived on the South Side, Providence's longtime ghetto. Either there or the West Side, which bordered it, the line between the two blurred a long time ago.

The bus had been silent when it had left Hendricken, as if it were leaving a wake, but now it was louder, full of teenage voices and occasional laughter.

"Keep it down back there," Nyblom yelled. "This isn't a victory party."

Kids could move on quickly after games; coaches could not. Nyblom was forever running the game around in his head as if it were some bad memory he couldn't shake, second-guessing himself, the endless torment of a coach. What could he have

done differently? Would it have made a difference? The endless questions in search of answers. Questions that have no
answers.

"Nyblom," came a voice from the back. "Right here."

The kids called him "Nyblom," even though he'd occasionally say, "It's Coach Nyblom, or Mr. Nyblom," though he knew
he had lost that little battle a long time ago, a battle that wasn't
worth fighting anymore.

The bus pulled over and a jayvee kid got out, wearing a dark
jacket and a dark hoodie. Then the chatter in the back started
up again, the voices getting louder. To me it was all background
noise, but apparently not to Nyblom.

"THAT'S IT!" he yelled, standing up and staring toward
the back of the bus, his face hard and rigid. "I don't want to hear
swearing, and most of all, I don't want to hear 'nigger.' People
have died in this country because of that word. People who
looked just like you were shot and killed because of that word.
It's one of the worst words in the history of the world. There are
people at Hope who went through hell because of that word—
teachers, older people—and I don't want to hear the 'N' word
again. It's completely unacceptable."

The bus went silent, and stayed silent until the last kid de-
parted.

"Why did we lose, gentlemen?"

It was the next afternoon, and the team was sitting at center court. Nyblom stood in the middle of them in his tan shorts
and dark blue sweatshirt, talking quietly.

"That is not a very talented Hendricken team," he said. "But
we didn't run, didn't get enough easy baskets. And we had a
couple of guys hanging their heads over lack of playing time. If
that's you, you have to ask yourself, What can I do to get on the
floor? What can I do to get more playing time? How can I be a

positive member of this team? Maybe it's bringing defensive intensity. Maybe it's taking a charge. You want to impress me?
Work hard. And do what you're supposed to be doing. That gets
my attention. That impresses me. That will get you on the floor.
Pouting on the bench will not."

It was an afternoon more of decompression than anything
else, coming down from the painful loss of the night before,
knowing there was a tougher game just two days away.

No one knew where Wayne Clements was. Johnson Weah
hadn't come to school. Delonce Wright hadn't come to school.
Neither had Manny Kargbo.

Neither had Dennis Wilson, a five-foot-ten senior with a
high fade hairstyle who had enjoyed some big moments the year
before, especially in the playoffs when he had helped Hope beat
favored La Salle with some key shots. But he didn't go to Hope;
he went to a school called E-Cubed, one of several charter schools
that had popped up around Providence in the past couple of decades. Most weren't big enough to field athletic teams; E-Cubed
students were assigned to play sports at Hope.

But the arrangement caused problems, not the least of which
was that Dennis was never around during the school day.

"He says he's staying after school over at E-Cubed to do
schoolwork, but the word is he's fighting with his girlfriend,"
Moors said, rolling his eyes, an expression that said you never
really know, even when you think you do.

Yet there were also rumors that Dennis's mother was thinking of moving back to Georgia. Whatever the reason, Dennis
had become another moving part on a team that already seemed
to have too many of them.

"BRICK CITY!" Moors yelled out as the team was doing
shooting drills, balls continually clanking off the rim.

"They can't shoot," he said to me, as we sat on the first row
of the bleachers. "They don't shoot enough. These kids don't go

to the playground and play all day like we used to. Ride around the city. There are empty playgrounds everywhere. Not like the old days. They're either playing AAU, or they're inside playing video games. Dave's here every morning on the treadmill at 6:30, so kids can come in and lift or go up in the gym and get up shots. But no one's there. They'll tell you how important basketball is to them, tell you how it's going to take them places, but you don't see them really getting after it. Ben, once in a while. Angel. That's about it."

Everyone is back the next afternoon.

So are the collective flaws.

The coaches still thought this was potentially one of the best teams in the state?

But if optimism was out there in the future somewhere, the truth was one of growing frustration for everyone: it was as if this were some pickup team that had first met at the playground about five minutes ago. There was no leader on the floor, and everyone was so imprisoned in his own individual universe that it seemed like the very idea of helping anyone else out was like a steep mountain no one had the tools to even begin to climb.

Johnson Weah was too interior, as though he were locked in a private world. Delonce Wright seemed to glide through life on his own rhythm. Ben Vezele was too quiet. Angel Rivera was too young. Manny Kargbo was too moody, plagued by whatever demons he was wrestling with, ones he didn't talk about. Wayne Clements was still not ready to play, showing up late when he showed up at all, and and then sitting by himself in the bleachers and looking at the treadmill in the corner of the gym as if it were the enemy.

And tomorrow they would face North Kingstown, a strong veteran team, in their first league home game of the season.

"I can't keep going over this, fellas," Nyblom said, as the first team couldn't run any half-court offense, even against the second team, never mind a real opponent. "You have to start thinking basketball. We can't keep doing this. We have turned the ball over almost every time down the court. Can somebody please make a simple pass?"

One player had red sneakers. Another had purple and gold. One player had black sneakers. Another had blue sneakers. It all seemed like cheap symbolism.

Play continued to deteriorate, and Nyblom's frustration grew.

"WHO'S IN THE LANE?" he yelled. "WAKE UP, ELI. . . . Get wide, Delonce. GET WIDE, DELONCE." Over and over it went in this old gym where the small banners hung down from the ceiling, and it was dark outside, dark and cold and already winter in New England.

A few minutes later the team was sitting on center court, sprawled on the floor like a defeated army.

"You have to start supporting and believing in one another," Nyblom said as he stood over them. "I want people to say, 'Resemble the basketball team.' I've got shirts. I've got sweaters. I've got ties. I've got whatever you need. Just ask."

He looked away, as if looking for something only he could see, then turned back.

"The problem is you don't know how to act. All you're trying to do is help yourself, when you should be trying to help other people, too. In this building I see people making fun of kids who are autistic. That is completely unacceptable, gentlemen. You have to learn to be a good person, a good teammate. You don't have to love each other, but you have to root for each other, gentlemen, and you have to respect each other. That's what being on a team is all about."

He paused.

"And you have to learn to make good decisions."

He pointed to a small kid with bushy hair named Anthony.

"Last night your father called me at 8:30 looking for you," he said. "You got out of practice at 6:30. I'm not going to lie for you. Be fortunate you have parents—or somebody—who cares where you are. Your parents are trying to set rules."

He paused again, looked at the kids sitting at center court who were looking up at him.

"There are still people here who are making bad choices, gentlemen. You have to be man enough to do the right thing. You almost can't watch the news without seeing some kid who is in the wrong place at the wrong time in this city who got popped. The sooner you get home the less chance that's going to happen."

CHAPTER THREE

It was December 14, Friday night, and Keith Moors was sitting in the cramped coach's office, the one where the clock always said 6:32.

"Home games are chaos," he said. "Dave and I do it all. We buy pizza. We buy soda. He sometimes hires a DJ. Something to jazz it up. Make it special. Because the school essentially does nothing. And it all comes out of our pocket. You just hope you get the money back. But you don't."

He shrugged.

"This job costs me money. Because I don't get paid. My second year I started giving out prizes. Little things. If you take a charge you get a T-shirt. Things like that. Dave and I run the concession stand, and anything we make goes back into the program. The DJ's a friend of mine. I pay him out of my pocket. How much does coaching here cost me? High end, $1,000. Low end, $500. Now the school wants the DJ to fill out forms. For what? They're not paying him. I am."

He ran his hand through his close-cropped black hair, the frustration on his face.

"The kids are always saying, 'What am I getting? What am I getting for free?' Dave tells them, 'I'm giving you free advice. Maybe you should listen.' But the amount of free stuff is unbelievable. The kids on SSI get free breakfast, free lunches, free everything."

He shrugged again.

"But the administration doesn't appreciate Dave here. They either don't know about all the things he does for these kids, or else they don't care. It's one or the other. And it's unbelievable to me. I've never seen anything like it."

When Moors had first come to volunteer he hadn't known what he was getting into. He just knew he wanted to be around an inner-city team, wanted to be around the game again, this game that had meant so much to him as a kid.

"I always wanted to be a social worker. Help kids. Something. You don't want to see them end up in jail. Or shot. So many of them need so much help."

Moors knows.

Once he was one of them. His father, who was black and lived on Camp Street, virtually in the shadow of Hope, was never in his life. His mother, who was white, was a drug addict, unable to deal with him. So he went to live with maternal grandparents in a white section of nearby Pawtucket called Darlington, a neighborhood to the north and west of Providence near the Massachusetts border. And it wasn't always easy.

"My grandparents were great with me," he said, "but I'd be riding my bike and cops would stop me, asking me what I was doing there. That stuff wears on you. I was the little kid with the big Afro in the middle of a middle-class white neighborhood."

When he was a teenager, his grandfather got sick. His grandmother couldn't deal with Keith by herself, and he was sent for a while to a group home in the northern part of the state. It was the first time in his life he was around a lot of minority kids on a daily basis, and it opened his eyes.

"I had started to be a bad kid when I was about twelve," he said. "Stealing. Getting in trouble in school. Hanging out with black kids from Prospect Heights in Pawtucket who always seemed to have loads of cash on them from breaking into houses. I wanted that. And I had no interest in school. I was in Special Ed for a while, spent time in what was called the 'time out room,' with kids throwing things. It was wild.

"But the group home was another league. I had never seen anything like it. These were kids that had it real bad. They couldn't go home. And every week I would come home and see my grandfather deteriorate. He was a tough guy, had fought in World War II. It was sad to look at. Eventually, my next-door neighbors took me in, and in a sense the neighborhood took me in. And when I went to Tolman High School in Pawtucket there were only a handful of black kids in the whole school. But I was used to that, and loved Tolman."

He played basketball at Tolman, never had a problem.

"I wanted to be the cool black kid," he said with a smile. "In the beginning I had to prove myself, a couple of fights, but after that it was all cool."

Then there was his father's side of the family, from Camp Street.

"Going over there was real different," he continued. "Kind of ghetto-y. Fire hydrants open in the summer. Hanging out on the corner. It was a cool place to hang out back then. But I saw it get real crazy. I've got a cousin whose house has been shot into something like twenty times."

Moors shrugged, as if in resignation. As if this were just the way it is, and there's nothing he or anyone else can do about it.

• • •

North Kingstown was a team from a big suburban town in the southern part of the state, a little more than a half hour away. They were a veteran team, one with legitimate state championship potential. The players had all grown up together, coming of age in various youth leagues in the way that happens in towns. So in many ways they, too, were the polar opposite of Hope.

"If you're not going to start and you are pissed already," Nyblom said, looking at Manny, "that is exactly the wrong approach. All it means is you've been doing the things you aren't supposed to be doing."

Manny looks disconsolate, staring straight ahead.

The team was in the Health Room, the tension starting to mount. This was the first real home game, a very tough test, and Hope was still unsettled, unformed, and unhappy. Their best player was being punished again, Wayne Clements was still not ready to play, and the team that was going to start the game was nowhere near the team the coaches had envisioned back in the fall. It all seemed fragile, as if the season had begun too quickly, and the best thing might just be to go back to the first day of practice and start all over again.

Last year Manny had come late to a home game, frantically running into the gym a half hour after the team was supposed to be there, but he still led the pregame cheers. Now he appeared crestfallen, the sadness etched on his face.

After the pregame huddle, and all the "Blue Wave" chants, and all the plans for getting off to a quick start, Hope was quickly down 11-2 in a crowded gym. A few minutes later the score had grown to 17-2. If it had been a boxing match Nyblom would have thrown a white towel on the court and it all would have been over. No such luck.

"It's all on you guys," Nyblom said in a time out, his face flushed, as if he were watching some horrible traffic accident.

"We're not slowing anything down. We're going to keep playing our style. If we get beat by forty we get beat by forty."

North Kingstown was in black uniforms; it was an experienced team that played like it. They had a quality senior point guard in Matthew Quainoo, their only black starter, a kid who seemed to be able to get anywhere he wanted on the court. They also had size and toughness, ran good offensive sets, were well coached, and played with the confidence of a veteran team that knew it was good.

In short, they were everything Hope wasn't.

By halftime it was 37-17, and Hope had already thrown the ball away sixteen times. There was an almost funereal silence back in the Health Room.

"There's nothing I can say to you, fellas," Nyblom said. "Keep playing like this and you won't even make the playoffs. There will be no URI. No Ryan Center. No nothing."

He took a deep breath, stared at his team. The players looked almost numb. Here they were at home, in front of all their friends, in front of several of the alumni, who no doubt looked at them in judgment. Here they were getting not just beat but publicly embarrassed.

"They outworked you and outplayed you," Nyblom went on. "They are slow and they are white and they are kicking your butts all over the floor. They're stronger than you, they're working harder than you, and they have more heart than you."

He stopped and stared at them.

"Because you have none."

If this were Hollywood there would have been a comeback for the ages, Hope charging back to redeem their tattered pride. But this wasn't Hollywood. This was the small second-floor gym of an old school on a cold December night in Providence, Rhode Island, a cramped, run-down gym where someone sat in a chair by the gym door and sold tickets for two dollars, and a table selling candy was a few feet away, and a Providence cop in his dark blue uniform stood in the doorway. And this was a team whose nightmare of a night wasn't finished.

Manny Kargbo played in the second half, but it didn't matter. At one point Hope was down thirty, Manny was back on the bench, and it had become garbage time. In the row behind him Wayne Clements sat in street clothes.

"Yo, Wayne, when are you going to come back?" Manny asked, looking at Clements, almost as if pleading.

"It's not me," Wayne said. "I'm not ready yet."

"We need a point guard, Wayne. I'm not a point guard," pleaded Manny. "I can't do it."

"It's not my fault," Clements said.

"But Wayne," Manny said, urgency in his voice. "We need you."

"That's enough," Nyblom said, standing up from the bench. "Now is not the time for this. After the game. Not now."

"Now you suffer the consequences of how you've been acting," Jim Black said to Manny.

"Okay," Nyblom said. "Everyone stops."

He looked at Manny.

"Either you stop now, or you go home."

Manny shrugged, looked back at Wayne.

"Him, too," Nyblom said, looking at Wayne Clements.

A few minutes later they were around the corner, down a short flight of stairs, and back in the Health Room, where the air smelled of complete and utter failure. Tuesday night against Hendricken had been a loss. This had been an embarrassment.

"There is something going on here that has nothing to do with basketball," Nyblom began. "You all think you are better than you are. You're jealous of each other, and on top of that you don't know how to play."

He took a breath.

"I wouldn't have picked you if I didn't think you could play. Last year, at their place, against the same guys, it was a great game. A great game. Tonight they kicked the living you-know-what out of you. Everything you want as a coach, they did. Us? We couldn't run any offense. We couldn't run any plays. Lack of effort? Lack of intelligence? You tell me. But is there anyone tonight who actually thinks he did anything positive in the game?"

The room was quiet, funereal.

"You have to take a hard look in the mirror and decide if you want to play or not," Nyblom went on. "If not, don't bother coming anymore. You argue with the fans. You argue with each other. You can't take criticism. You pout when one of the coaches says anything to you. And you can't talk to each other positively. It can't go on. It just can't. Tuesday night at Hendricken we played with intensity. Tonight we played with nothing. Tonight was an embarrassment. You embarrassed the people who were here to watch you. You embarrassed the former players who were here. You embarrassed the coaches. Most of all? Most of all, gentlemen? You embarrassed yourselves."

He turned around for a second, as if finished, then turned back again.

"So go home tonight and think about it. And if you still want to be a part of this team you will be here by ten o'clock tomorrow. No excuses."

Nyblom looked drained, beat up. And when he spoke again, his words were coated with emotion.

"And if you want to be on this team then you bring your lunch pail and start working hard. If you do that, fellas, we will be fine. If you don't start to believe in yourselves and your teammates you will go nowhere."

People had begun lining up in the hallway of the Rhode Island Convention Center in downtown Providence at 10:30 in the morning. They came in all sizes and all shapes on a bright, cold Saturday morning ten days before Christmas. The convention center is in the middle of a complex that was the symbol of the Providence Renaissance in the '90s, adjoining both the Omni Hotel and the Providence Place Mall. On the other side it's connected to the Dunkin' Donuts Center, the twelve-thousand-seat arena that had opened in the fall of 1972. It's where Providence College plays its basketball games, as do the Providence Bruins, the American Hockey League franchise and the premier farm team of the Boston Bruins.

It is an impressive complex, and when it opened it had given a well-needed shot of civic pride to an old downtown that seemed so rooted in the past. But the people lined up in the hallway were the other Providence: poor, nonwhite, wearing discount-store clothes, waiting for a holiday meal sponsored by the Rhode Island Food Bank. Many of them were old and wore the look of poverty; they'd never gotten the memo about the Providence Renaissance.

The Hope team came into the hallway in their dark blue warmup suits. They looked almost like royalty, young and strong and happy in a hallway full of old people with forlorn expressions on their faces as they waited in silence for the doors to open.

"This is Team Building," said Moors quietly. "It's Dave's idea. We did this one day last year when we were off to a miserable start. Manny was being Manny, Delonce came to us and said we were yelling at them too much. So we stopped yelling for a while and then we were 2-7 and we said the hell with it and went back to yelling.

"But one Saturday we had no basketballs in the gym. Guys came strolling in late and we passed out brooms and mops and cleaning supplies. The kids couldn't believe it. But we all mopped the floor, cleaned the backboards, went outside and picked up trash in the courtyard. Kids hated it. But they did it. And that seemed to turn everything around."

"Right now they're all I, I, I. Me, me, me," Nyblom said. "Hopefully, they can get something out of this."

He had already held a little pow-wow with Manny earlier in the morning, for he knew the situation was reaching the breaking point. He also knew that Manny's home life was not easy, knew that Manny's mother worked three low-paying jobs, his father was living in Delaware, and he had a complicated life for a senior in high school, even without basketball and the inherent pressure that came with that. He also knew that, in many ways, Manny Kargbo was a fragile personality, often held hostage by his emotions, yet beneath it all just a kid trying to find his way in a new country.

Now Manny was standing in a hallway, frustration all over his face.

"I can't even sleep," he said emotionally. "This is my senior year. We have to be better than this."

He looked away.

"I get sidetracked. I get distracted," he said softly, anguish in his voice, "I have trouble focusing. My mother has problems. My father has problems in Delaware. But I can't be yelling at my teammates. I know that. I have to take a leadership role. I have to act like a captain. I have to be a leader."

I felt a certain affection for Manny.

He had been the first Hope player I'd met. That was the spring of 2012, when I was first thinking of following Hope through a season, and Nyblom had dropped him off one afternoon at the *Providence Journal*, right across the street from where he was now standing in the convention center. It had been his first extended interview with a reporter, and I wasn't asking him how he took the ball to the basket that afternoon, but about his journey from the besieged Liberia of his childhood to a high school basketball court in Rhode Island.

We sat in a small conference room that afternoon and he said he had started playing basketball in Delaware when he was twelve years old, and at the beginning everyone was better than he was. But he kept going to the nearby playground to try to learn this strange new game in this strange new country.

In the summer of 2009 he came to Providence with his mother and his younger brother, Titus, who now plays for another Providence high school, on the other side of the city. They had come to Providence because his mother's younger sister was here. They moved into the Hartford Avenue projects on the west side of the city, a tough, grim place run by the Providence Housing Authority that could be the setting for a contemporary Dickens novel.

"I didn't know anybody," he had softly said that day. "I just thought that was what life was."

For the first time in his life he began to get serious about basketball, sometimes even shooting by himself in the rain on the outdoor courts, as if the courts were a sanctuary of sorts, a place where he could lose himself for a while in this strange new game he was trying to learn, this game where you could shoot by yourself and play imaginary games in your head that could take you out of your own life for a while. But when he went to Hope as a freshman, thinking he was going to play soccer, an older kid he only knew as Mookie said, no, he was going to play basketball and that was that.

Not that he was any good in the beginning. He was a stranger from a strange land in a strange new country. He said that in his first jayvee game he was horrible, and in his first varsity game as a sophomore the next year he had been terrible, and it wasn't until the following summer that he began to get a lot better.

He told all this softly that afternoon at the *Providence Journal*, and afterward I had driven him back to the East Side and dropped him off in the small parking lot in the back of Hope.

"Thank you, sir," he had said as he got out of the car.

So I didn't like to see the obvious pain he was in, for I had come to know there was nothing malicious about Manny, even on these days when he so often appeared sad and moody, as if the weight of his world were sitting on his shoulders, just underneath his T-shirt.

Inside the cavernous convention center there were innumerable tables with white tablecloths and red napkins, for the people would get a meal in addition to some clothes. The Hope players were waiters, moving from table to table. They were smiling, happy; they seemed so different from the night before in the Health Room after the game. Once the people had been seated, a Catholic priest said a benediction, one that ended with the words "pushing back against the darkness in our world, giving us hope in a world where there is always hope."

Even in a high school basketball season for a school named Hope?

That was the question after the North Kingstown debacle.

That was the question with a league record that was now 0-2 and starting to resemble that of too many Hope teams that had come before, talented teams whose seasons had collapsed from self-destruction and dysfunction.

Manny was the biggest key, certainly, but by no means the only one. There was little question that Hope needed Wayne Clements back if they were going to be able to turn this mess around, but it was beginning to seem like a sports version of *Waiting for Godot*. He was forever coming in late to practice when he showed up at all, seemingly doing little to speed his recovery so he could get back on the court. He would ride the stationary bike in the corner of the gym for a while, then go sit by himself in the bleachers, occasionally making a comment or two, but removed, both physically and emotionally. Hope desperately needed a point guard who could run a team and make everyone better. Angel Rivera, though not without talent, was just a sophomore, not experienced enough, not yet ready to lead a team that started three seniors—Manny, Johnson Weah, and Delonce Wright. It was as though Wayne had simply checked out, not just in the gym, but in his own world, too.

On a Tuesday night in South Kingstown, a large town in southern Rhode Island that borders the Atlantic Ocean and includes the University of Rhode Island on its northern side, Hope readied itself for another game.

It was the same gym Nyblom had played in as a senior at South Kingstown High School back in 1981, when he had been one of those blue-collar, do-everything guys, the kind of guys who are great teammates, guys Nyblom always was trying to get his players to become.

South Kingstown figured to be a run-of-the-mill Division I team, a mix of a few returning veterans and some promising younger players, a team Hope was supposed to beat if they were anywhere close to being as good as they thought they could be. During the jayvee game the Hope players sprawled on the dark blue bleachers behind the Hope bench. There was no crowd to speak of, and Angel Rivera was sitting in the front row saying he had no idea where he was.

"You're near the University of Rhode Island," I said. "Near the beach. Near Narragansett."

He nodded.

"I think I went there once."

Angel was five-foot-eight on a good day, with close-cropped dark hair and a wonderful smile that lit up his face. He had tattoos on the backs of both arms, and wore bright orange sneakers with his dark blue warmups. He had been born in Puerto Rico, came to Providence when he was three, moving into the Chad Brown housing project. He still lived there, with his mother and three sisters. His father lived in Boston.

Chad Brown is in the northern part of Providence, just a few hundred yards away from one end of the Providence College campus. It's named after the Reverend Chad Brown, one of the founders of Providence and one of the first ministers of the city's historic First Baptist Church on North Main Street, which separates downtown from the start of College Hill and the East Side. He had arrived in Rhode Island after being exiled from Massachusetts for religious reasons, just like Roger Williams, the state's founder.

Chad Brown was Providence's first low-income housing project, opening in 1941. It had been established by the Wagner-Steagall Act of 1937, Franklin Roosevelt's attempt to demolish slum neighborhoods and beautify them by creating public housing. The idea had been that public housing would become a utopia where all social classes would come together, but only fifteen years after it began public housing was being referred to as "the projects." When it first opened, there were 198 units in Chad Brown, built as row houses, which originally housed six hundred people. But by the end of the '60s it was overrun by youth gangs and inhabited by the poorest of the poor, mostly nonworking families, mostly all headed by single women. Nearly half a century later, little has changed. Students from nearby Providence College are told to avoid Chad Brown.

One guy on a website called "Go Prov" recalled seeing dumpsters set on fire, cars flipped over, and rampant drug dealing. "They're nuts over there," he said.

Now Chad Brown has the reputation of being one of the worst housing projects in the city. Forty years ago in a national magazine it had been called one of the three worst housing projects in the country. A story in the *Providence Journal* in the summer of 2012 mentioned that it always seemed to be dealing with routine shootings, rampant drug dealing, and random car fires. Since the year had started there had been roughly 170 reported incidents of domestic assault, vandalism, and larceny, and there were two homicides and eight robberies with a firearm. There were street-side memorials to those who had been killed. The story also said that when kids hear "East Side is here," they know to run from possible gunfire.

"How old were you when you heard your first gunshot?" I asked Angel.

He thought for a second.

"About ten. Maybe younger."

He looked away for a second, then turned back.

"But the violence has died down."

"Why's that?" I asked.

"All the bad guys are in jail."

Angel didn't start playing basketball seriously until just a few years ago, growing up with football and baseball. But now it's basketball. When he envisions his future, he is playing basketball at a college somewhere.

"I want to play college basketball as far as it can take me," he said, his eyes on the jayvee game going on in front of him.

Why not?

College basketball was some mysterious Land of Oz that hovered in the future. Not the college of classrooms and studying for exams, or the idea of walking across a green college quadrangle on the way to a seminar taught by an esteemed professor. Not even the idea of graduating and using the degree as passport to a better life. Nor was it the idea of parties and going to football games on sun-splashed Saturday afternoons. College meant college basketball, the way it is presented almost nightly in the winter on ESPN and Fox Sports, the college basketball of frenzied fans and Dick Vitale's voice, the idealized image of big games and the magic of the NCAA Tournament in March, cultural messages as powerful as dreams.

Sitting nearby was Wayne Clements, in a big blue shirt that seemed a few sizes too large for him.

"It's very difficult to watch the team play knowing I can't play," he said softly.

"So you want to play?"

"Yes, I want to play."

"This team doesn't need a point guard as much as it does a leader," I said. "Can you be that?"

"Yeah."

He looked out at the jayvee game.

"I knew a lot of them before I ever got to Hope."

"How's that?"

"From rec leagues. From Sackett Street. I've known Marquis and Ben for a long time. You grow up in the city and you're always playing against the same people. That's just the way it is."

"How's your knee coming?"

"It's getting there. But everyone thinks if you don't play you're not tough. It's not like that. I tore my MCL."

"So you don't like everyone saying that you're taking too long to come back?"

"No, I don't like it."

He paused.

"When I can play, I'll play."

I changed the subject, trying to keep the conversation going.

"What's your favorite subject?"

"I don't have a favorite subject."

"Do you ever study?"

"Not really. Unless it's a big test."

"Are you going to graduate?"

He looked away again. Was he envisioning his diploma in the ceremony downtown at Veterans Auditorium in June? Was he envisioning what would happen if he didn't get one?

"I'm going to graduate," he said.

"So it's no problem?"

"Not really," said Wayne Clements, with a shrug.

Hope was down by one at halftime, in another game in which no one could score, as though someone had simply put in a tape of the Hendricken game and hit the "play" button. Same story. Same outcome. Hope always in the game, but not winning, now 0-3, with another postgame locker room full of frustration and angst.

"This is a huge moment right now, gentlemen," said Nyblom, "and you have to decide how we're going to get better. We had twenty turnovers. We keep missing layups. That's why we're 0-3. But it's more than that. You screw off in the classroom. You chase girls after school, or else go down the street to McDonald's instead of studying and doing what you're supposed to be doing before practice. That's why we're 0-3 too."

He went around the small locker room, pointing to one player after another.

"You're pissed because you don't play . . . you're pissed because you don't get enough shots . . . you're pissed because you're always pissed."

As he took a breath, Jim Black pointed to Wayne Clements, who was standing in the corner.

"If you are waiting for him, you won't have a season," Black said forcefully.

Then Pedro Correia spoke, something he rarely did in the varsity locker room. But all the kids respected him. Not only had they played for him on the jayvee team, in many ways Correia was Hope High School, outlasting countless principals and innumerable teachers. He was the one who had played for Hope, back in the early '70s in the first years of busing in Providence, when everything had started to change. He was the one who knew the kids who had played thirty years ago, the institutional memory. He was the one whose roots went back to high school basketball in Rhode Island for forty years, having played against Quenton Marrow's uncle, a great player at Central High School, the best high school basketball team in the state at the time. In retrospect, that Central team had been a harbinger of the future in the Interscholastic League, an all-black team that pressed all over the court. Correia was the one who knew Hope in ways nobody else did.

He had grown up on Camp Street, back when, as he put it, "You didn't have to worry about getting shot. I never had any fear living there." But he had long since come to know how different things were now, saying that "I wouldn't want to be a kid today," recalling the early '90s when the gang violence began to hit inner-city Providence like the flu. One day he gave one of his players a ride home to South Providence and the kid got out of the car with a hood over his head and ran down the street because there were people who wanted him dead.

When he spoke he did it quietly, but everyone listened.

"You may never play on another organized team again," he said. "But you come late. You have bad habits. You don't do what you're supposed to do. You guys are blowing a great opportunity. You are only going to be at Hope one time in your life."

The coaches walked out of the small room.

Almost as soon as they were gone, Manny and junior big man Quenton Marrow were in each other's faces, their voices heated.

"But I'm the captain," Manny said loudly.

"You don't act like it," Marrow shot back.

"You should do what I say," Manny said.

"Why?" Marrow said, not backing down.

"Because I'm the best player," Manny said, as if he couldn't understand why Marrow couldn't understand his logic.

"But you don't act like a captain," Marrow shot back.

"But I am," Manny said, frustration in his voice.

On and on it went, the conversation heated, the other players watching, saying nothing.

Suddenly, the coaches were back in the locker room.

Nyblom looked at Manny and pointed at Quenton.

"This kid is polite, respectful, and always does the right thing. He's the one that's always taking the balls downstairs at the end of practice, making sure they're all in the locker room so they don't get stolen. He's the one who's always supportive and enthusiastic on the bench, while the rest of you pout and sulk when you don't play. He's the one who acts like a captain."

He paused.

"Look, fellas, I don't mind tension and I don't mind anguish. No one should be happy when we lose. I'm not happy. The other coaches aren't happy. And I don't mind you venting. Because I'm going to vent, and you can vent too."

He pointed at Ben Vezele, the thin six-foot-four junior, who could look so graceful one minute and disappear the next.

"You're wasting this year. Because right now you're physically incapable of doing what you want to do. You have the ability to be our best player, but you have to get in the weight room and you have to get stronger."

Nyblom paused.

"Do you have anything to say?"

"Manny never admits he's wrong. He won't listen to anybody," Vezele said.

Dennis Wilson looked at Wayne Clements.

"You have to get yourself to practice more," he said.

No one else said a word, the gloom and despair hanging in the small locker room like a bad odor. Their record was 0-3.

CHAPTER FOUR

Hope was built in 1936 in the middle of the Depression with money from the Works Progress Administration, one of the federal projects created by President Franklin Delano Roosevelt to get the country up and moving again. It rose across the street from the Hope Street High School, an old red-brick school that had been built in 1898. The new school was set on land that had been a public reservoir since 1875, complete with a stone pump house on its north side.

It was a showplace when it opened, one of the largest high schools in the country, big enough to accommodate 2,200 students. It had sixty classrooms, an auditorium that could seat over a thousand kids, a library, a modern cafeteria that could accommodate seven hundred at one sitting, a gym, a smaller girls' gym, and a locker room big enough to have 105 individual shower stalls. There was a music room and a music library. There was a machine shop, a woodworking shop, and a metal shop. There were two white cupolas on top of the brick school that gave

Hope, from a distance, anyway, the look of an impressive building in the middle of an Ivy League school. Hope was completed
in June 1936, at a cost of $1,995,748 dollars.

And until the late '60s, by all accounts, it was a school that
worked; it was the very definition of a large, comprehensive high
school of the era. Students were assigned to one of three tracks—
college, commercial, and vocational—often moving through
their days as if in three different parallel universes, only coming
together for home room, lunch, and physical education classes.
This was the era of academic "tracking," a time when everyone
going to college was not the goal. Most of the kids came from
the East Side and Smith Hill, so in many ways it was a neighborhood school, even if there were exceptions.

Hope won the state basketball title in 1961, a team that finished 26-0, then advanced to the New England Tournament,
played on the famed parquet floor in the old Boston Garden
where the world champion Boston Celtics of Bill Russell and
Bob Cousy reigned. Hope lost in the semifinals to Wilbur Cross
of New Haven, Connecticut.

The star of the team was Al Lopes, a thin, silky-smooth
light-skinned black kid. He was six-foot-six and had grown up
as one of ten children in his family, who lived in the Fox Point
section of Providence, down past Brown at the south end of Hope
Street, but less than a mile from Hope. The other black player
was Norman Lambert, a skinny six-foot-four kid who also came
from Fox Point and lived with an older woman known as "Miss
Tillie," a foster parent. The other forward was Carlton Chace, a
white kid from Washington Park in South Providence.

The two guards were both from Smith Hill, the white
working-class neighborhood less than two miles away, but not on
the East Side. It was a neighborhood of narrow streets and wood
triple-deckers in the shadow of the Rhode Island State House, a

white domed building that looks out over downtown Providence to the south. One guard was Henry Giroux, who would go on to teach at Boston University and Penn State, among other colleges, write over fifty books, and be called by one website one of the fifty most influential progressive educators in the world.

The other was Tom Cannon, who went on to be a college teammate and lifelong friend of Jim Calhoun, the Hall of Fame basketball coach at the University of Connecticut. Cannon was the crafty point guard, a product of the very strong Catholic Youth Organization basketball culture in Providence at the time. In an era when no one had ever heard of AAU basketball, innumerable city kids learned the game in the CYO leagues that were all over Rhode Island at the time. Cannon played for St. Patrick's on Smith Hill, always one of the top CYO teams of the era, one coached by a man named Joe Hassett, whose son, Joey, would grow up to star for nearby Providence College and later play in the NBA. Hassett was one of those old-school coaches of legend who coached for the sheer love of it, for there was no money, not much recognition, and certainly not many tangible rewards involved.

It was a more innocent time, of course, a time of Sadie Hawkins dances and poodle skirts, of letter sweaters and dances in the gym. In 1961 Vietnam was still in the future. Drugs were in the future. The counterculture was in the future. So were many of the things that would divide America by the end of the decade. High school was its own cocoon then. And if there was occasionally something on the nightly television news about "sit-ins" in the segregated South, it could have been happening on the far side of the moon for all the players knew.

"We never had a racial problem," Cannon said. "Not one. We were all teammates. Hope was really a melting pot back then. A lot of blue-collar kids. But it worked. It was a good school."

The Hope coach was Mike Sarkesian, one of those tough

taskmasters the era all but had a patent on. It was Sarkesian who helped his players go to college, and when he heard that Lopes was enlisting in the Air Force he went down to the induction center and said, no, this kid is not going into the Air Force, he is going to college. After Lopes spent two years in a junior college in the Midwest he went to Kansas, where he played with future NBA player Jo Jo White on a team that came within a basket of going to the Final Four in 1966. It's a famous game in college basketball history, as White was called out of bounds after making a shot that would have beaten Texas Western, the Cinderella school that upset heavily favored Kentucky in the championship game to win the national title, the little school no one had ever heard of that started four black players and was immortalized in the movie *Glory Road*.

"Mike Sarkesian changed my life," Lopes recalled, having become a lawyer in Lawrence, Kansas, far away from the Hope of his childhood. "My only other option was to go into the Air Force and come home and work for the city like everyone else in Fox Point did back then. So many kids now have the wrong idea of what a basketball scholarship is. Basketball is supposed to be a means to an end, not an end in itself. It's gotten out of hand. It's frightening, actually. Basketball gave me an opportunity, and I took advantage of that opportunity."

All five of the starters on that '61 Hope state championship team went on to college.

The team was a mix of different kids, diverse before anyone knew what the word meant. The school was, for all practical purposes, a neighborhood school. So there were the Jewish kids from the East Side who didn't go to Classical, the academically elite high school where there was a quiz a day in every subject. There were the working-class kids from Smith Hill, who, while not on the East Side, lived within walking distance of Hope. There were the black kids from nearby Camp Street.

There were the Cape Verdean and Portuguese kids from Fox Point. And there were the other neighborhood kids from the East Side, many of them Jewish. All together in a big red-brick building on busy Hope Street that had two white cupolas on its roof, a building that once had been a showcase but now was starting to show both its age and all the effects of nearly three decades of teenage feet scuffling through its halls.

By many standards of measure, Hope was a success story for different kids with different aspirations. Ed Shein, who had started high school at Classical, transferred to Hope, and ended up going to Brown, remembers that many of the black kids spent much of their time on the second floor, where the shop and commercial classes were, almost as if they attended a different school. But every year there were kids who went off to nearby Brown or to some of the other finest colleges in the country.

And the sports were great—not just basketball. A state title in hockey, where Hope played at the Rhode Island Auditorium a mile or so away on North Main Street, which ran parallel to Hope Street going north. Great in track, where famed Rhode Island high school coach Bill Falk routinely sent his stars to colleges all over New England. To look through a yearbook from the early '60s is to see a very traditional high school from that era, the boys in long-sleeve shirts and khaki pants and short hair, the girls in skirts, their hair often styled. Yes, it was the '60s, the beginning of them, anyway. But the '60s that defined the decade, the time that began to change America in ways that were unfathomable back then, were still off in the distance.

"It was a wonderful building then, and a great school," remembered Jerry Kapstein, who played football and baseball and graduated in 1961. He then won a scholarship to Harvard, became a lawyer, and began a lifelong career in sports, including being the CEO of the San Diego Padres and the senior baseball advisor to the Red Sox, among other things. "My father had graduated in 1935, where he had been a big football star, my mother in '36. As a kid I had always had wanted to go to Hope.

"There were never any racial incidents. Lummer Jennings, who was black, was the class president and I was the vice president. We had great teachers who cared about us. It wasn't a good school. It was a great school. I mean I liked Harvard. But I loved Hope."

Then came court-ordered school busing.

Busing arrived on top of the tumult of the mid to late '60s: the growing anti-war sentiment, the beginnings of the rise of the counterculture, the start of the Civil Rights era, the gurgling cauldron that would come to define the '60s. No high school was immune then, especially one that was in the shadow of Brown, and just a couple of hundred yards away from the heart of Thayer Street, symbolic ground zero of youth culture on the East Side. Look at a yearbook from the late '60s and you might not recognize it as being a representation of the same genre of universe as the one that had existed just a few years ago. White boys with long hair. Black boys with Afros. White girls with long straight hair. Black girls with Afros. And everywhere there were the accoutrements of the growing counterculture, from the ragged clothes to the obvious disdain of anything even perceived to be conventional, all the signs that change was everywhere, and that it wasn't just the answers that were blowing in the wind.

It wasn't just change; it was dizzying change.

Busing began in Providence in 1969, as a response to what a professor of education at Rhode Island College had called "decades of indifference at best and powerful opposition at worst." Part of that sentiment, in retrospect, was that Providence always had housed a small black population. In the early '60s the black population in the city's schools was roughly 17 percent. In 1966

Hope had the largest percentage of black students of any high school in the city, at 15 percent.

The tumult of the late '60s was challenging many of the old orders, and one of them was the schools. From curriculum to tracking, and from facilities to student expectations, everything was under attack, everything was being questioned. There were committees, studies, open meetings, innumerable stories in the *Providence Journal* about an antiquated school system in crisis.

And in April 1969 it all blew up at Hope.

The Bus Stops Here, the 1974 book by Anna Holden that chronicles the turmoil of three American cities, including Providence, describes one example: "Hope black students went on a 'rampage' through the school—smashing windows, lightbulbs, and furniture, assaulting some teachers and white students, and doing extensive damage . . . fire extinguishers were emptied and flags were ripped and burned. . . . The Hope rampage was the first outburst of its nature in Rhode Island and greatly shocked many whites."

The '60s had arrived at Hope, and the ramifications would last for decades.

"We called it Hopeless High," said Steve Waldman, who went there from 1971 to 1975.

He grew up on the East Side, the child of parents who had both attended Hope. But the Hope his parents had known and the one he went to were two different worlds.

"It was a pretty intimidating place," he said. "It had probably twice the student population it has now, a big monster."

Waldman had gone to middle school at Nathan Bishop, an old brick building across the street from the Brown football stadium and in the heart of the residential East Side, stately brick homes just a street or two away. Nathan Bishop had been roughly one third black then, mostly kids from Camp Street, but nothing had prepared him for what he was about to see at Hope.

"Busing had started a couple of years before I got there, and there were a lot of Italian kids from the North End who were bused there every day, and the black kids from South Providence who also were bused in. They were like oil and water. Always fighting. And every year there would be a race riot. It would always be in the spring. There would be one at Central High School one day, and one at Hope the next. The white East Side kids would be hiding under tables. Or standing up against the walls with their trays up over their face. Nathan Bishop had been a mixed place, but people essentially got along. Hope wasn't like that. Some of the black kids would go up to white kids and take their ice cream sundaes right out of their hands. Or else take their ice cream cone, give it a lick, then hand it back. It was an intimidating place."

Waldman also remembered Hope as an old facility in the early '70s. He had grown up hearing his parents talk about Hope being a friendly place in the '50s, how the black kids had gotten dressed up for dances, how there was "no racial stuff." The Hope he encountered was the opposite.

"I never went to a sporting event in all the time I was there," he said, before adding that a couple of the basketball games back then were played in a "closed gym," code for no spectators allowed, for fear of violence. "It just wasn't a friendly place. The racial stuff always hung over everything."

But the worst thing he ever saw at Hope?

"I had a math class up on the third floor, taught by an old guy who must have been a hundred years old, and a handful of black kids would terrorize him every day. They would make jokes. They would always fool around. They would sit there and read the paper while he was trying to teach. And one day—no word of a lie—they tied him to a chair, held him by his feet, and threatened to throw him out the window. He was shell-shocked. I've never forgotten it."

He looked away, as though searching for a memory.

"I don't know if I've ever been back there since I graduated," Waldman said. "I don't even think about it when I drive by, and I have driven by it thousands of times. I have no emotional connection to it. None. It's just another old building."

He looked away again, as if he were looking all the way back to the early '70s.

"Busing was supposed to lift people up," said Steve Waldman softly. "Instead it sucked everything else into the sewer."

CHAPTER FIVE

That was forty years ago, but in many ways little had changed, save for the fact that the building had gotten older. It was all but impossible to spend any time inside Hope and not be constantly reminded of both its age and that it had become another city school that no one seemed to have any faith in. A few years earlier it had been divided into three mini-schools, each with its own principal, and each with its own supposed theme. Hope also had adopted so-called block scheduling, which meant the classes were appreciably longer, ninety minutes instead of the traditional forty-five or so.

On the surface it might have seemed like an educational version of rearranging the deck chairs on the *Titanic*. But, if nothing else, it made things more orderly. Or as one of the school's social workers explained, "There's always the potential trouble when everybody's in the halls. That's when things happen. So having less hall time makes things better, regardless of anything else."

By all accounts the new system had improved Hope.

But even though both faculty and students liked it, the block scheduling system was abolished in 2010, supposedly so all the public high schools in the city would be uniform. That spring scores of students walked out of Hope during the school day and marched downtown to City Hall to protest, to no avail.

To the coaches, though, this was all politics.

They were always fighting the things that transcended both the politics of the building and the various educational philosophies that seemed to be constantly changing. Hadn't Nyblom been through something like nine principals and countless vice principals in his twenty-four years? Hadn't he learned that, at some level, teaching was simple? Wasn't it all about doing the right thing?

That was at the heart of his message. Be on time, work hard, do what you're supposed to do, care about others, be a good teammate. These were the lessons he had grown up with, coming of age in southern Rhode Island as a "swamp Yankee," the name given to people who often were "land poor," people who believed in old-fashioned values like family, faith, and helping others, people who had both a strong sense of place and of doing the right thing. All those timeless qualities that long ago had become the articles of his faith. All the truths that had survived all the years and all the educational theories. All the things he kept stressing every day, which the culture outside his gym so often seemed to oppose.

So he looked at the fact that there were some Brown students at Hope every afternoon offering to tutor students. He looked at the resources that were available to kids that too often weren't utilized. He knew there were nights when parents could meet with teachers about their child, but only a handful would show up in a school of roughly nine hundred students.

That was Nyblom's ongoing frustration, this sense that so

many kids could be significantly helped if they—or their parents—would just listen to those trying to help them.

He had seen it get worse in the past couple of decades. More kids with social problems. More kids with academic problems. An appreciably smaller school than when he had first started, more Latino now, where twenty years it had been more African American. A lack of respect for adults. Words like "motherfucker" and "nigga" accepted parts of the language in ways they never were before. An increased sense of entitlement. The fact that the overwhelming majority of fights at Hope were between girls. The increasingly transient nature of the school population. More poverty, more kids wearing the same clothes every day. More and more kids in gangs, even the ones you would never have imagined as gang members. The fact that so very few kids ever got picked up after road games when the bus come back to Hope, the sense that so many kids were on their own.

This was Nyblom's world, one he had seen get more hard-edged and complicated the longer he'd been at Hope.

"Dave's going to have to send a couple of these kids packing and it's going to kill him," Moors said one afternoon during another lousy practice where the coaches were all but yelling into the wind. "These kids are different. There's such a 'me' attitude. Wayne cares about Wayne. Manny truly believes he's a Division I player, but he doesn't sleep right. He doesn't eat right. Doesn't live right. Doesn't ask anyone for help. And all the people hanging around him, all the people always telling him what he wants to hear? They think he's great. And he thinks he has control of the team because he's a senior and he's the best player, but nobody listens to him."

Moors shrugged.

"But his mother works three jobs, and his father lives in Delaware and is in and out of his life, so it's not like it's easy."

The practice going on in front of him was typical: Nyblom frustrated, Wayne Clements not around, all the flaws on display. Corey Brinkman, the only white kid on the team, a football player who was trying to play basketball in his senior year, had realized he was simply too far behind the others and had quit. So had a skinny Hispanic kid Nyblom was always calling Ricky Rubio—in reference to the flashy NBA player from Spain—to the point that I had never learned his real name. He was just Ricky Rubio.

"We're averaging thirty-four points a game," Nyblom said loudly. "My son's rec team gets that by halftime."

"This is making me sick watching this," Moors muttered. "We go down to South Kingstown and spend half the time playing like we're scared. Hope High School was never scared. People were scared to come here. When my brother played here in the '80s people would be lining the walls here. Crowds were crazy. They intimidated teams. They were a tough city team, and other teams around the state were scared to come in here. There would always be cops all over the place. Now we're the ones who seem scared. I don't know what happened. Playing soft? This is Hope High School. We can't be soft."

"STOP FOOLING AROUND AND BOX SOMEONE OUT!" Nyblom yelled. "WE CAN"T KEEP DOING THIS."

He whistled and everyone stopped. He called them to mid-court.

"Gentlemen, we can't keep doing this," he said, softly now. "One game we played well, even though we lost. The others? We haven't played well at all. We have to get stronger. We have to get quicker. We have to get better ball-handling. And there's no magic formula. The only way to do it is to put more time in.

"And gentlemen, the coaches can't keep screaming and hollering at you all the time. You have to do it. You have to figure it out together."

The players stood silently.

"You have to figure it out—and the other kid who's not in the gym today? He's got to figure it out too. You have to figure out why you don't go to the weight room. You have to figure out why you don't get more shots up every day. Because that's what good teams do. Teams that want to win, that's what they do."

He stopped, and looked at the players standing around him, as if to somehow make sure they were hearing his words, really hearing them.

He pointed at Aaron Lynch, a six-foot-three senior who was new to Hope this year, having moved to Providence from Connecticut with his father.

"You are a wonderful kid, Aaron," he said. "But you have to get stronger."

He pointed to another kid, who wore a dark headband.

"If you don't learn the plays I can't use you."

He pointed to junior Devante Youn, a rugged six-foot-three forward.

"Two years you've been trying to get in shape. I don't get it."

He looked around at all the players.

"It comes with a sacrifice, gentlemen. We can't make you do it. Today's practice was a waste of time. I didn't see anyone bust it. You play as if you don't want to be here. It's bad, fellas, it's real bad."

And it didn't get any better against Cranston West on a Friday night before Christmas at home. Nyblom's last message to his team in the cold Health Room was that they all needed a Christmas gift, a win to get things moving in the right direction.

"Be a leader," he said, pointing to Manny. "And yelling at people is not being a leader. Let me do that."

But soon they had lost their way, another ugly, low-scoring

game that was like a rugby scrum down the stretch, another game that could have gone either way, until it went Cranston West's, in another heart-wrenching defeat.

"Are you ever here?" Nyblom said to Wayne Clements as they walked down the small set of stairs that led to the Health Room.

"You blaming me?" Clements asked.

"No, I'm not blaming you," Nyblom said. "I'm trying to get you to help us."

Once again, the room smelled of failure and defeat. Once again, the players had forlorn looks on their faces. All except Manny Kargbo, who walked in carrying a box of popcorn.

"You should be here every day," Nyblom said to Clements, shaking his head.

He turned back to his team.

"Last year was last year. I don't know if we're still trying to live off that. We had a great tempo out of the gate tonight and then nothing happened. And we can't keep turning the ball over. It's killing us. We had twenty-three turnovers tonight and that's just too many. No one really did anything bad, but we just don't do enough positive things."

He turned to Johnson Weah, who sat at a table with his head in his hands.

"Look at me. Don't get down. We need your effort. We need your hustle."

He stopped, took a breath.

"Pick a day next week when we're on vacation," he said to everyone. "Come down to the house. We'll spend the day. We'll figure it out. . . . We should be 3-1. Shoulda. Woulda. Coulda."

Nyblom was calming down, almost visibly coming down from the emotion of the game. Then he saw Manny sitting in front of him with his hand in the popcorn bag.

"Do you really need to be eating that popcorn?" he said

sharply. "Because I told you not to. So do you really need to be putting on another show? Like the one you put on the other night in South Kingstown yelling at everyone? STOP EATING THE POPCORN."

It was the day after Christmas, a Wednesday morning, and there was no heat in the gym. There also was no Angel Rivera and no Jeremy Rivera, the two supposed cousins who both lived in Chad Brown on the other side of the city, and no Dennis Wilson, either.

Last year Wilson had made some big shots in the state tournament at the Ryan Center at the University of Rhode Island, but so far he'd been a nonfactor, missing half the time. It always seemed to be something. Girlfriend problems. Working with a teacher after school at his charter school on the other side of the city. Something. Providence has four public high schools, but now there are also over a dozen charter schools, most too small to have their own athletic teams, so their athletes are dispersed to the four traditional high schools.

"What's up with Dennis?"

Nyblom shrugged.

"He says his mother is moving back to Georgia."

Nyblom's affect was that's just the way it is, as if he had long ago tried to stop worrying about things he can't control. As if that were the only way he could survive emotionally in a school where there were always so many things you couldn't control. But on a team that couldn't shoot there was no question that Hope was a better team with Dennis than without him. Nyblom still had expectations: Wayne's knee would get better, and Manny would get himself emotionally straightened out, and Dennis would start to make some shots, and Ben would get tougher, and Johnson and Delonce would find their basketball legs after football, and Hope would be the team Nyblom kept believing they could be, as good as any team in Rhode Island. But he had come to know that it's always fragile, a delicate basketball ecosystem that can self-destruct at any minute, a team that had started out 0-4, even though some of the key pieces from the team that went to the state finals last year were still here.

To Nyblom, though, there was no real mystery to it. You got better by putting the work in. You got better by working hard in practice. And if there was no heat in the gym on a cold winter morning? Well, that was part of it too.

No one had ever given him anything. His father had worked for the Recreation Department in South Kingstown, one of those guys who went to work every day, no questions asked, because that was what being a man was all about. So this is what he knew, what he always had known. And when he had come to Hope in the fall of 1989, such a different world than the one he had grown up in, he brought the values of his childhood with him: work hard, treat people with respect, do the right thing. The varsity coach at the time was Jerry Morgan, a black man from Gary, Indiana, who first had come to New England in the early '60s to try out for the New England Patriots, then landed in Providence, where he played in the fall for a semiprofessional football team called the Providence Steam Roller.

It wasn't long before Morgan came to realize that the largely segregated Indiana of his youth, where blacks and whites essentially grew up in different worlds, in many ways had been better than what he was seeing in Providence with its de facto segregation.

"Most of our families were intact, and we didn't have drugs and guns," Morgan said.

Nyblom had learned from Morgan. Saw the way he dealt with kids: tough on them, but always giving them another chance, too.

"We need to score points, gentlemen," Nyblom said now as

the team scrimmaged. "Shoot the ball. . . . I don't care if you miss a hundred shots in a row, Ben, we need you to shoot. . . . SHUT UP AND PLAY. . . . You want to get on the floor, Devante? Play harder. . . . You keep playing like this, Eli, and you'll get on the floor."

Eli.

His name was Elijah Lewis, a skinny little left-handed sophomore guard with a high fade haircut and an often bemused look on his face, as if he couldn't quite believe what he was hearing. He was from Bridgeport, but his mother was originally from Providence, so here they were, not that anyone seemed to know why. This, too, was Hope: kids coming and going, transferring in, transferring out, for all kinds of reasons. One kid on the team had attended Mount Pleasant, another city school, but after being threatened by a classmate there he was moved to Hope in what was called a "safety transfer."

In the beginning Eli seemed ticketed for the jayvee team, just another young kid with potential, but now he was flying around the court as though he were on skates on a smooth sheet of ice, darting here and there, making plays, an obvious talent.

"Someone wants more playing time," Moors yelled out. "You keep playing like this, Eli, you'll never get off the floor."

This was a graphic reminder to everyone in the gym that starting lineups weren't chiseled in stone, that the roster was like the stock market, players moving up or moving down. That, too, was Nyblom's coaching style.

It was vacation week, so everything was a little looser, a little less structured; some kids were away on break, or who knew where. It was one of Nyblom's fears, the sense that his players had too much time on their hands, offering the potential for trouble. He liked it best when they were in the gym, days with some structure. There were roughly thirty-five gangs in Providence, with roughly two thousand people identified as gang members, according to the *Providence Journal*. They were the kids Nyblom used to see hanging on the corners years ago when he drove Laurence Young home, the kids in school one day and gone the next, now "on the street," code for they probably were never coming back.

This was Nyblom's reality, the world he lived in every day, so he had become extremely sensitive to what was happening to his team's psyche. Who seemed troubled? Who seemed to be drifting? Who has having trouble in school? Who had girl problems? Who might have something going on at home?

One person who seemed different in the gym, but in a good way, was Manny Kargbo.

"He's torturing you, Quenton," Nyblom yelled to Marrow. Manny was getting to the rim anytime he wanted. He also seemed happier. He had come back from Christmas with a new haircut and a new attitude, almost as if they had been presents under the Christmas tree. He smiled. He talked to both teammates and coaches, engaged in ways he rarely had before, emerging as the Manny everyone had been waiting for.

"You should have been with me yesterday," said Moors, coming over and sitting beside me in the first row of the bleachers. "There was a jayvee tournament at Mount Pleasant. We lost to St. Ray's by thirty-four. One kid got locked out of the gym. Another kid got taken out and went behind the bench and took his shirt off. It was awful. Kids mouthing off. One kid got taken out and goes to sit a few rows back with a couple of the varsity guys who were there watching. Another kid got taken out and started taking his sneakers off. And the kids that don't start, or get taken out of the game? They sulk."

Two kids came into the gym in street clothes, one about six-foot-five, the other shorter.

"Look at that sad story," Moors said.

"Who's that?" I asked.

"That's Shaq," said Moors.

Shaq.

His real name is Shaquille Jones, and I had been looking to do a newspaper story on him for a couple of years. Once he had been one of the state's rising schoolboy stars, right there with Ricardo Ledo, who in the spring of 2013 was chosen in the second round of the NBA draft, even though he had never played a minute of college basketball. But then Shaq Jones had left Hope to go to Notre Dame Prep, in Fitchburg, Massachusetts, nudged there by Leo Papile, the founder of the Boston Amateur Athletic Club, one of the showcase AAU teams in the country, which has sent innumerable kids off to college kids in the past thirty or so years of its existence. Notre Dame Prep is one of those places in the basketball world where a lot of lost souls go in search of that nirvana called NCAA eligibility. To Jones, it was a very different world from the one he had grown up in just off Camp Street on the East Side.

"I was always around bad things as a kid," said Jones, who grew up with his grandmother, a woman who used to sometimes ride the Hope bus to away games when he was playing there. "My friends were criminals, breaking into people's homes, stealing cars. But I wasn't like that. I was trying to be a father figure to my younger brother, because I didn't have a father figure. And I had older kids who protected me, told me basketball could take me places, that I had a gift for it."

In many ways, Jones was an inner-city stereotype: an absent father, a mother who was in and out of his life, being raised by his grandmother, a lost kid trying to use his basketball talent to give himself a better life. The basketball world is full of them, of course. Some are the ones we see on television, the winners in the great basketball lottery. The ones we don't see? They still periodically show up in their old high school gyms, looking for futures they never found.

Jones had been on a team full of college prospects at Notre Dame Prep, far away from Hope and the Rhode Island Interscholastic League. In his mind, he and his teammates were all on the same fast track to a college basketball world of loud cheers and TV games, the fantasyland dangled in front of kids as if it's some magical kingdom.

"I loved it," he said softly. "You had to go about your business, and I grew up from that. I was a starter, and I knew I was going to college."

Then his girlfriend in Fitchburg got pregnant.

He said that last February he'd been thrown out of school for what he calls a "campus incident." He stayed in Fitchburg for a while with his son's mother. Now he's back in Providence looking to get his GED with hopes of going off to a junior college next year. He's only nineteen.

So now he was sitting in the first row of the bleachers watching practice.

"What would you tell those kids out there?" I asked.

"I'd tell them to listen to the coaches. Not be hard-headed," he said.

He nodded at Nyblom, who was on the court running the practice.

"Me and him bumped heads," he said softly. "I would get frustrated."

He looked away for a second, and when he spoke again his voice seemed to come up through layers of regret.

"But now I know that my dreams were his dreams too."

CHAPTER SIX

It was December 31, a morning practice.

"Gentlemen, there is no heat in the building today," Nyblom said, words of welcome.

No matter.

Manny was in Delaware with his father. Dennis was not at practice. Nor was Devante Youn. Nor did anyone know the whereabouts of Anthony Ortiz, a little-used reserve.

But Wayne Clements was in the gym, an unexpected post-Christmas gift.

"Hey, let's have a cheer," smiled Nyblom as Clements walked over, his hair in cornrows, his thin body wrapped in a dark sweatshirt that was too big for him.

Wayne was wearing red sneakers, and as the players jogged around the gym to get warmed up he was last, just going through the motions.

"He's a dog already," laughed Moors, as Nyblom smiled and shook his head. "He's the biggest dog there is. But you know something? Our season's going to start to turn around. Just watch."

Also in the gym were Shaquille Jones and his younger brother, Josh, who would be a senior now at Hope if he hadn't gone off to a New England prep school. He, too, was a visible reminder of how ephemeral everything was. That was just the reality, one that Nyblom had long ago learned to let slide off his back. The Jones brothers were just two examples: two brothers who had grown up about a jump shot away from Hope but who hadn't lasted four years there. One more big opportunity for a great season gone.

"How's the team doing?" Josh Jones asked Moors.

"Oh-and-four," he said.

"Oh-and-four?" Josh Jones said.

"You know how it is," Moors replied. "They don't listen for the first two months."

Josh Jones laughed.

The Jones brothers went off to get ready to scrimmage against the team.

Moors watched them go, a faraway look on his face.

"Shaq was on that team two or three years ago when two of our kids were arrested across the street at Moses Brown for stealing some laptops when we went over there to play them right before the season started," he said. "All they had to do was admit it and the whole thing probably would have been dropped. But they kept denying it, even though they were on tape and the cops had the tape. We were loaded that year. But they got suspended for a couple of games and everything fell apart. That could have been a state championship team. We were devastated.

"But Shaq was something special, and he knew it. That was his problem. Now he's humble. And even though he's been gone for a couple of years Dave's going to try and help him out."

Two more alumni walked into the gym, began warming up.

One was Malieke Young, with the orange streak in his Afro. And it was quickly apparent that there was something larger going on than just an unofficial scrimmage between the Hope team and some guys who once had played for Hope. It was a sort of family reunion, but extemporaneous and genuine. Nothing organized, nothing structured. It was a statement of tradition in a school that had lost sight of it, this big, inner-city school where so many kids seemed to come and go as if through a revolving door, a statement that being on the basketball team had been important in ways that maybe hadn't been appreciated at the time, as if this were their connection to the school.

This, too, was Nyblom.

For they were his kids forever, no matter what had happened when they'd been at Hope, no matter what they were doing now, no matter how difficult they might have been when they'd played for him. The door was always open. Bygones were bygones. He would always make calls for them, always try to help them.

"Throwback Monday," yelled out Moors.

It was January 2, a new year, but the same season.

It was late afternoon and Nyblom sat in the cluttered phys. ed office. They were getting ready to play at Woonsocket, and the kids were eating pizza that Nyblom and Moors had bought.

"I've been texting Dennis all week," Nyblom said, "saying we had a game. He finally texted back today saying he'd be here."

But he wasn't.

The other kid missing was a little backup guard who had quit, claiming family problems.

Nyblom shrugged.

"Sometimes seven or eight kids are better than thirteen or fourteen," he said.

The players popped in and out of the phys. ed office,

grabbing more pizza. This was dinner, for the players lived too far away from Hope to go home after school and then turn around and come back for the bus to Woonsocket, a trip that for most of them would have taken four buses.

It was after four when they boarded the yellow school bus at the back of the building for the roughly half-hour trip north. The bus went up Route 146 out of Providence, with both the varsity and the jayvee team crowded inside. By the time the bus got to Woonsocket it was getting dark and cold, early January in New England.

With a population of just over forty thousand, Woonsocket is the sixth biggest city in Rhode Island, another old mill city whose glory days seem in the past, a victim of changing technology and a bitter economy. It's been a city since 1888, and was the longtime spiritual home of the French Canadians in Rhode Island, at one point home to a French-language newspaper and radio programs and movies in French. But the Depression in the '30s ravaged the city, and fifty years later there was still high unemployment, and its small downtown seemed like a tired monument to the past. The city's only sports glory came from the parochial Mount St. Charles hockey team that had dominated Rhode Island high school hockey for decades.

Woonsocket High School, tan and sprawling, on the outskirts of downtown, looked like it belonged in the suburbs. Inside, there were red and orange walls, the corridors clean and well lit, as was the gym. The locker room had orange and yellow lockers, and was so clean you could have eaten off the floor. The Woonsocket players were mostly all nonwhite, as were most of the hundred or so people in the stands. The coach was Kyle Ivey Jones, a six-foot-six black man who had grown up on Long Island and had played at the University of Rhode Island in the '90s. In the internecine world of Rhode Island basketball, everyone knew who he was.

Inside the Hope locker room Marquis Young and Aaron Lynch were in a rap contest, standing up and quickly trading lyrics as if they were punches, until Nyblom quieted everyone down.

"We're 0-4 and Woonsocket is out there laughing and joking, because they think they're going to beat us," he said. "So this game is going to come down to three things: decisions, effort, intelligence. If you want to fool around and chuck up three-pointers and not get back on D, we will be in trouble."

The players sat there in their dark blue uniforms with the gold trim.

"But I'm worried about what we're doing," Nyblom continued. "We've got to run more. Rebound better. Stop chucking up three-pointers, because we're about ten percent shooting them. We've only scored fifty points once, and that just puts too much pressure on the defense. We're losing to teams we should be wiping the floor with. So let's start to change it around starting tonight."

He took a deep breath, and just stared at them, this big man in his dark blue short-sleeve shirt that said "Hope" in gold letters over the pocket.

"We believe in you, gentlemen," he said softly. "You have to start believing in yourselves."

A few minutes later I was sitting in the bleachers with Bob Whalen, the father of volunteer assistant coach Rob Whalen, who had played basketball at Hope in the early '60s. He had grown up on Smith Hill, a blue-collar working-class neighborhoods of wooden three-deckers in the shadow of the State House that overlooked downtown. He came to all the games, one of the small handful of people who did.

"Hope was fantastic then, a great, great, school. Jewish people. Black people. White people. Everyone got along. I loved it," he said.

He nodded in the direction of the court.

"This makes me want to puke."

He had seen too much of the arguing and the finger-pointing, the players going down to the other end of the bench and sulking when they were taken out of the game, the periodic displays of blaming each other when things went wrong, the obvious dysfunction that all too often seemed to be part of the lineup. Now it was a couple of kids fooling around, as if they were getting ready to play a pickup game instead of a league game they desperately needed to win.

A few minutes later the players came back into the locker room for one more mini-meeting before the game was due to start. But everything had already changed, all the good feeling of just fifteen minutes ago gone.

"You guys just don't get it," Nyblom said disgustedly. "Half-court shots. Fooling around. It was embarrassing. We had a decent week of practice and then you come out and act like this. We're 0-4. This is a game we need. For it's all slipping away, fellas. And you just can't turn it on and off. Because right now you're just going through the motions. And you guys have to figure it out."

By the time the game started there were a couple of hundred people in the stands and with 7:30 left to play in the first half the score was 10-10, as neither team seemed able to do anything. By halftime Hope was up five, but nobody seemed able to make a shot, and the frustration was all over Nyblom's face.

"That team stinks," he said loudly back in the locker room. "They don't have ball handlers. They don't have shooters. But guess what, fellas, the only reason we're ahead at all is they've missed ten free throws."

"People are laughing at you," Moors said.

Throughout much of the second half Nyblom had Manny, Ben Vezele, and Delonce Wright on the bench. He went with Johnson Weah as his big man, surrounded by four little guards in Angel and Jeremy Rivera, Eli Lewis, and Khalil Robinson to hang on to a 54-46 win.

"Give yourselves a hand," Nyblom said afterward. "Manny, Delonce, and Ben were all terrible and we still won."

The players were putting their clothes on over their uniforms as Nyblom continued to deconstruct the game for them.

"Look, Johnson," he said to Weah. "I love your hustle. I love your attitude. I love everything about you. But you have to play smarter."

He looked around the small locker room.

"Tomorrow, gentlemen, we're practicing right after school. So if you get detention you'll be late. And tomorrow I will look over everyone's progress reports. But right now? Right now we got a win."

"That's right," ' Moors said in a loud voice, "0-4 IS OVER."

In the middle of all this a black kid from Woonsocket walked through the meeting as if he were walking through his own living room, oblivious to what was going on around him. Nyblom watched him and just shook his head.

"One more thing," Nyblom said as the players began to move toward the door with their traveling bags. "If I were you guys I'd be real pissed at Wayne Clements and Dennis."

CHAPTER SEVEN

Four days later Hope was due to take another bus trip, this time to Charlestown, Massachusetts, the tiny city of one square mile that sits in the shadow of Bunker Hill, seemingly no more than a jump shot away from the Boston Garden and downtown Boston.

It was a brilliant sun-splashed Saturday morning. The night before, Hope had lost at Coventry, in another game they could have won but didn't, another game where they hadn't played well. So now their official record was 1-5, and a season that had started out as a disappointment was now close to turning into a disaster. The discontent was everywhere.

The loss had followed two days of desultory practices after the win over Woonsocket, ending any hope that that game was going to miraculously change the season. The first practice had come with the news that Dennis had finally quit, done in by too many personal problems that had weighed him down from the start of the season.

"His choice," Jonathan Weah said tersely.

But they all knew they were better with Dennis, for on a team where nobody seemed able to make two jump shots in a row, Dennis could. Or at least he had done so the year before. Manny had missed one practice with an excused absence, Nyblom seemed preoccupied with bad school progress reports, and any bump they had gotten with the win in Woonsocket seemed negated by the loss at Coventry. If nothing else, a 1-5 record in January was digging a deep hole, the kind that had the potential to bury a season before it had had a chance to begin.

So the mood in the cramped phys. ed office before the bus to Charlestown showed up was gloomy at best.

"I came into coaching with ideals," Pedro Correia said, almost forlornly. His jayvee team had been terrible so far, but it was more than that. It was the sense that something important had been irrevocably lost, not just on the basketball court, but in a generation of kids who seemed clueless, cast adrift in a rudderless society whose obstacles the kids were powerless to overcome.

"But it's all so different now. Because you have to lower your ideals. You have to be flexible in ways you never had to be before."

"The street gangs are worse than anyone thinks," said Moors, who worked for years as a guard at the state prison in nearby Cranston. "You see that in the prison system. They come in with their gang bond, which is why they take pictures of all your tattoos when you get into the prison system. Then they become friends with people inside who have shot some of their family members. The whole thing's unbelievable, just so sad, for so many of them are just kids with no clue. But on the outside they've all got guns. And there's a lot of gunfire in Providence every night. It's just not all reported."

But some of it certainly was. It had become all but impossible to pick up the *Providence Journal* in a given week and not see story of street violence, the type of story that once would have been a rarity. I had lived much of my adult life in Providence and had always found it a very livable, safe city. That had changed, as had the city's perception. There had been too many news stories in the *Providence Journal*, too many grisly images on the television news. The city was tougher now, and many of the urban ills were getting more and more difficult to avoid.

A few minutes later the yellow school bus left the parking lot and headed down Olney Street to I-95 and the start of the hourlong ride from Providence to Boston.

I sat on the bus with Quenton Marrow, the thin six-foot-five junior with black-framed glasses who had gotten into the argument in the locker room with Manny after the loss in South Kingstown earlier in the season. There was something different about Marrow. He always dressed well. He was always friendly, open, in ways many of the other kids were not. He also seemed more grounded than many of the others, in that he had no desire to be a professional basketball player, the stereotypical fantasy of so many inner-city kids.

"I want to be an electrician," he said as the bus drove up the interstate.

He lived on the South Side, across the street from Ben Vezele and close to Wayne Clements and Marquis Young, and had gone to Roger Williams Middle School. He had wanted to attend Classical, the longtime academic jewel of the Providence school system, but didn't get accepted. So his next choice was Hope, where two of his older sisters had gone, even though most mornings he had to walk, since he lived 2.8 miles from Hope, just two tenths of a mile away from being eligible for free bus passes. And since his father lived in Boston, and his mother recently had been laid off at work, he couldn't afford to take the bus every day.

He said how, at some level, he regretted the verbal spat with Manny in the locker room after the loss at South Kingstown, but that he had to let his frustration out, that he had kept it bottled up for too long. He wanted the team to do well, and it was all but driving him crazy that Manny hadn't been acting like a captain.

When he first got to Hope he was surprised by how many fights there were, and by how one kid had recently been arrested for having a weapon in school. He said there had been a lot of fights recently, and just yesterday there had been a fight between two Latino kids. Most of all, though, his experience there had taught him an indelible lesson.

"The stuff that happens at Hope doesn't happen at Classical," he said.

The bus was getting closer to Boston when Marrow said that it gave him hope when Barack Obama was elected president, because he saw how happy it made his mother, and it also gave him hope that maybe things could change. The family plan was to leave Providence in the summer of 2014 after he graduated, to go to Virginia, where his mother's family is from. So he was preparing to go to college there, another example that Quenton was more grounded than most of the other players.

"What do you know about Brown?" I asked, for I knew that so many of the Hope kids, including him, walked by it every day, in their trek down Thayer Street to the bus tunnel that went downtown to Kennedy Plaza, where the buses to the varying parts of the city originated.

"Not much," he said.

"How about if I told you that it's one of the most prestigious colleges in the country and there are kids who come from all over the world to go there?"

He looked at me.

"I didn't know that," he said.

He looked away for a second, out the window, before turning back to me.

"I've heard they have a good cooking school," he said.

No matter that Marrow was getting Brown confused with Johnson & Wales, a different university in Providence that did have a good cooking school. It was a sad reminder how little these kids knew of so many things the rest of us in Providence took for granted, how disconnected they were. Not only was Brown the seventh oldest college in the country, but its hockey rink and gym were literally less than two hundred yards away from Hope, to the point that you could stand on the corner of Hope and Lloyd Avenue outside the Brown hockey rink and feel as if you could almost touch the high school. So it almost defied belief that so many of these kids were clueless about what it was, and what it represented, even though there were Brown students who came to Hope nearly every afternoon to help tutor Hope kids. It was as though the Brown students and the Hope ones lived in distinct parallel universes within a few hundred yards of each other.

The bus was moving through Boston on this bright winter day, now on the Tobin Bridge, having just passed the Boston Garden, where both the Celtics and the Bruins play.

"Have you ever been to the Garden?' I asked.

"No," he said.

Off in the distance, on the other side of the Charles River, was Harvard, visible in all its splendor in the noontime sunshine.

"What's the most prestigious college in the country?" I asked.

"Harvard?" he asked, the question in his voice.

"You're right, Quenton," I said. "Do you know where it is?"

"Not really," he said.

"It's right there," I said, pointing out the window.

"Really," said Quenton Marrow, with a big smile on his face.

· · ·

Charlestown High School sits in the shadow of the Bunker Hill Monument, complete with its own tortured history, one of the centerpieces of the Boston busing crisis in the early '70s that was all over the network news at the time, a time of racial unrest in this old city referred to as "the Athens of America," the city of Lexington and Concord and Paul Revere, this city whose history was intertwined with America's. It was racial unrest, with all its ugly fury, and it had shocked the country at the time. For this wasn't some southern backwater; this was Boston, "the city upon a hill," the city that had featured the country's first public school as far back as 1865, the city that had spawned the anti-slavery movement, women's rights, civil disobedience, and the philosophical movement known as Transcendentalism.

If the first battleground in Boston's racial crisis then was South Boston, a white, ethnic, Irish working-class neighborhood that erupted when black kids from other parts of the city were bused in to achieve racial balance in the schools, as mandated by federal law, Charlestown had been the second battleground. It had begun September 8, 1975, the morning of the first day of the new school year. And making it all the more horrific was that it was happening outside a high school in the shadow of the Bunker Hill Monument, a 221-foot granite obelisk that had been erected in 1843 to commemorate the Battle of Bunker Hill, the site of the first major battle between the British and the Patriots' forces in the Revolutionary War. This had been one of the most famous battles of that war, remembered by schoolchildren for one of the most famous lines in American history: "Don't fire until you see the whites of their eyes." Charlestown was also the place that had been represented in the U.S. Congress both by John "Honey Fitz" Fitzgerald and his grandson John F. Kennedy. It was in the northern section of Boston, one square mile of narrow streets, three-deckers, and bars, and now in many ways it's been gentrified, discovered by the Yuppies, who love its proximity to downtown, its rehabbed old buildings, and its newfound city charm.

Inside the Charlestown High School gym, red championship banners from 2000, 2001, 2002, 2003, and 2005 hung on one wall.

Because it was a nonleague game, one that didn't really affect Hope's record, the vibe was a little different, as if everything had been turned down a notch. But for a team that was now 1-4 in the league with its season close to imploding, it was all about getting better before it was too late. But this time Nyblom didn't coach; he sat one row behind the bench as Moors coached. The gesture was Nyblom's way of not only giving Moors more game coaching experience, but also letting his players hear a different voice. Once again, Hope wore their dark blue road uniforms with the gold trim and "Blue Wave" in white on the front of the jerseys.

Hope showed very little energy in the pregame warmups. It was the afternoon, there were maybe fifty people watching in seven rows of bleachers, and Hope had played the night before. Loud rap music was bouncing off the walls. Charlestown wore blue warmups with red-and-white trim and looked like a real team; they had the kind of size you didn't see in the Rhode Island Interscholastic League. It figured to be a long afternoon.

Then it happened.

The Manny everyone had been waiting for was on full display as if he suddenly had turned into a mini–Dwyane Wade in the prime of his career. He went through Charlestown. He went around them. He was unstoppable in the open court, finishing at the rim with both hands. He did it over and over, taking the ball inside against bigger guys and scoring over them. And just when it seemed Charlestown was going to survive the blitz, he would do it again. He finished with thirty-six points in a thirty-two-minute game, as Hope held on to win 72-69, by far their best performance of the season.

"That's the first time we've seen Manny all year," said Pedro Correia afterward.

But as great as he was, he wasn't the entire story for Hope. For Wayne Clements finally made his comeback.

He had started the game, and from the beginning it was quickly apparent that he made Hope a better team. A point guard who didn't play in a constant frenzy, he provided instant stability. Moors called him "the forty-year-old point guard," and in many ways he was right on target. There was something very old-school about Wayne as a basketball player, as if in a speeded-up frantic basketball world only he stayed under control. He wasn't extremely quick, and he didn't have exceptional speed, but he definitely knew how to play, no insignificant thing in a basketball world where too few kids knew how to, even the talented ones. He handled the ball well. He changed speeds. He made the right pass. And he could make open three-pointers, something no one else on the team could do with any regularity. Since the season had started, all the coaches agreed that Wayne Clements would make the team better.

He did.

And coupled with a happy, focused Manny, he helped the team play like the one the coaches thought Hope could be.

"That was fun," Nyblom said afterward in a joyous locker room. "That's the way basketball is supposed to be played. No yelling at each other. No talking back to the coaches. No sulking. Playing the right way."

The game had come at exactly the right time. There had been too much losing, too much discontent, too much frustration. This had been sheer, unadulterated fun, everyone getting into the game. A win, complete with the smiles and the sound of laughter afterward. It spoke to many things, of course, not the least being the resilience of youth. Forgotten was the loss to Coventry the night before. Forgotten was the record. They had won a game and on the bus ride out of Boston in the gathering dusk, all of the realities of the season had been momentarily forgotten. Hadn't Tolstoy said that all happy families are alike? So are winning basketball teams.

A half hour later the bus was halfway down I-95, on the way back to Providence, the back of the bus full of noise and laughter, when the word that most infuriated Nyblom could be heard.

"ENOUGH," Nyblom said, getting out of his seat in the front of the bus and staring into the back of it. "I DON'T WANT TO HEAR THAT WORD."

"You know what the biggest joke is?" yelled Moors to the back of the bus. "We're still 1-5."

The next afternoon I sat in the coffee shop of Old Mountain Lanes in South Kingstown with Nyblom. It is across the street from the recreation complex where his father fell off the back of a truck while attempting to fix one of the basketball hoops and died shortly afterward. Nyblom was twenty-nine at the time and had never imagined his father dying so suddenly.

"It was devastating," he said.

In many ways he had enjoyed an idyllic childhood. All four of his grandparents had been alive, and came to his games when he was a kid. His paternal grandparents had owned season tickets to the University of Rhode Island basketball games at Keaney Gym on the nearby University of Rhode Island campus, and they often took him along. He played football, basketball, and baseball as a kid. Later on, he spent summers unloading fishing boats on the nearby docks in Galilee along the southern Rhode Island coast and worked at basketball camps. Most of all, he learned the lesson he's always carried with him, the lesson that runs through his coaching philosophy: treat people the way you want to be treated and you'll never have a problem.

He knew early that he wanted to be a phys. ed teacher and a coach, so when the first job opened up in an elementary school in Providence he took it. That eventually led to one at the Roger Williams Middle School in the heart of inner-city South Providence, and two years later to the job as a physical education teacher at Hope.

"All I really knew about Hope then was that it was inner-city, and they were good athletically," he said.

It was 1989 and Hope housed roughly fifteen hundred kids then, as many as six hundred more students than it has now. There were only four public high schools then in Providence, not the thirteen there are now, including smaller schools and charter schools. And from the beginning he liked Hope. But now it was nearly twenty-five years later and time had not been kind to the school. The heating system was old and needed constant attention. There was a water pipe problem, complete with a sub-basement that was often full of water. Hope was wearing its age. It had been seventy-seven years since Hope opened as a showcase school that was all about the future. To Nyblom, it had long ago become a money pit. Administrators come and go, and so do educational philosophies.

"Many of the kids come in here with reading and writing skills at the sixth- or seventh-grade level," he said.

He has also seen the racial makeup of Hope change dramatically, going from roughly 60 percent African American when he first arrived to roughly 60 percent Hispanic now. But to Nyblom, it wasn't just the racial makeup that was different, it was the culture, too. The girls who want to get pregnant. The kids who arrive in need of significant academic help. The kids who can't sit still in class. It was the fact that most of the fights at Hope are girl fights. That boys put pictures of themselves doing something illegal on Facebook and wonder why they get arrested. It was the fallout from rap culture, in which entertainers who are cultural icons to kids sing about guns and slinging drugs and going to jail. It was the gang signs—the "tags"—that were everywhere, if you knew what you were looking for. In short, it had all the problems that come from a society in crisis.

"Jeremy is a father to be," Nyblom said.

No wonder he's not always around, I thought, another kid who has far greater realities to deal with than how much playing time he gets.

"We have six hundred kids who come every day to first lunch in the cafeteria," Nyblom went on, "and five hundred leave their stuff on the floor. African kids arrive here in this country and they're very polite. They come here and everything changes."

And most of all, there were the kids he knew who didn't make it, for one reason or another. These were the ones that haunted Nyblom, all the little tragedies through the years, the ones he will never forget, the ones in the future he's always trying to save, right there on his personal scorecard. For he saw many more gangs now than when he started, especially in the past five years. Some members were kids he never would have suspected, good kids dragged in by peer pressure and other reasons, and so much of the conflict was over nothing, this street against another street, lives ruined over an address. He has had kids who were terrified of cops, kids who saw them as the enemy. He has had kids who used terms like "nigga" and "motherfucker" as common speech, a vulgarization of the language that was the result of both rap music and a popular culture that glorifies street culture.

This was his world, and it was one that some of his friends have never understood, always asking him after too many beers,

"How can you coach those kids?" It was a world of disconnected phones and changed addresses, kids who always seemed to be moving, as if change were a shadow they could never shake. And it was the guys in the black community who questioned him, like this fuckin' white guy doesn't know what he's doing, what's he doing coaching Hope? Most of all, it was all the drama that was right there on the scoreboard somewhere, the drama that never seemed to go away. Like the time he ended a season with just seven players, though that was fine with him because those seven did the right things.

It was a world he'd lived in for a long time now.

But he knew he'd paid a price for it, too. He lived in South Kingstown, thirty-five miles south of Providence, with his wife, Tammie, and their two kids, in the same family compound he'd grown up in, and his days were long, leaving the house at six every morning and returning over twelve hours later, as he also coached girls' soccer in the fall. He had missed many of his own kids' activities through the years, events he knew he would never get back. But he still loved what he did every day, because it was all he'd ever wanted to do.

CHAPTER EIGHT

Hope's next game was against Mount Pleasant, another big red fortress of a school that had been built with WPA money in the same era as Hope. It was across the city on the west side, in a residential neighborhood that bordered Triggs, the city-owned public golf course that had been designed by the famed Donald Ross. And it was next to Rhode Island College, too, a mostly commuter school that has been in Providence for half a century. But if Mount Pleasant once had been a middle-class school in a middle-class neighborhood, now it was an inner-city school in a middle-class neighborhood, beset with many of the same problems Hope faced.

Mount Pleasant's assistant coach had been one of my inspirations to spend a year following Hope through a season. His name is Tom Conner, and I played pickup basketball with him for years. In March 2012 I had done a newspaper column on him, specifically what it's like to coach an inner-city basketball team year after year.

"People have no idea," said Conner, a former All State high

school player who is white, and has coached high school teams in Providence for nearly two decades. "They have no idea what our kids go through just to play on a team."

Like Hope, Mount Pleasant had several kids who went to other schools, but played basketball for Mount Pleasant.

"Just getting to the building every day is an accomplishment," he continued. "So is getting home. Because they come from all over the city. Playing here is a major commitment. They start out with two strikes against them. They get here by themselves. They go home by themselves. The parents are never around; you almost never see them at games. It's not easy. I have a tremendous amount of respect for these kids."

I had already come to have the same feelings about the Hope kids, for it hadn't taken me long to see that it wasn't easy playing for Hope, for the same reasons Conner had expressed. There wasn't much student support at games, certainly not like in a suburban school. There was hardly any community support, save for a few older guys who once had played. No one lived close enough to walk home, so all were on two buses afterward. There were no cheerleaders. No pep band. None of the pomp and circumstance we so often associate with high school sports. In all the important ways they did it for the love, and maybe the idea that it had the potential to take them someplace they could never get to without it, the basketball dream that hovers over every high school in the country.

There were rarely any parents at the games, save for Wayne Clements's father, who came to most of the home games, and Aaron Lynch's father, who came to a handful. Nor were parents waiting when the bus returned after road games.

One night, after one road game early in the season, I was on my way out of the small parking lot behind the gym when I saw Jeremy Rivera talking on his cell phone at the end of the larger parking lot near Olney Street. It was cold and dark, and he didn't seem to be to wearing a winter coat. I asked him if he needed a ride.

"Someone was supposed to pick me up, but they're not answering," he said.

"No problem," I said. "Get in."

He said he was going home, and I knew he lived in the Chad Brown housing project a couple of miles away, over on the western side of the city near Providence College, the same place Angel Rivera lived.

"Are you and Angel really cousins?" I asked, trying to make conversation.

"We're name cousins," he said.

A minute later I heard him on his cell phone.

"Yeah, I'm getting a ride," I heard him say.

He was silent for a couple of beats.

"The book dude."

One of the Mount Pleasant players was Titus Kargbo, the younger brother of Manny. He is bigger than Manny, roughly six-foot-three.

"So why isn't he here at Hope?" I asked Manny in the locker room about an hour before the game.

"I guess he wanted to compete against me," he said with a shrug.

Oh.

Manny was on earphones, listening to a three-hundred-pound rapper called "Big Pun." The team was down to thirteen players, in their white home uniforms with the blue-and-gold trim. And, as they had for most games, everyone wore different-colored socks, plus a few had different-colored sneakers—blue, orange, red—as if little statements of individuality.

The gym was packed, complete with six policemen. Three stood on one end of the gym, three on the other; they didn't represent a menacing show of force, but were a presence none-theless. As Moors said, this was a "city game." Wayne Clements was again in the starting lineup, and quickly threw an around-the-back pass on a fast break for a layup, then made a three-pointer, two more quick examples that Hope was better when he was in the game. But in many ways it was a typical inner-city game, rough and physical, with both teams having trouble scoring. Hope led 23-13 at the half, despite having thirteen turn-overs and going 1-8 from the foul line.

"BLUE WAVE, BLUE WAVE, BLUE WAVE," the play-ers chanted, as they huddled up before the second half started, their arms on each other's shoulders, as they slowly moved back and forth like one large body.

They went on to win 58-48, after being up twenty-one points with a little under eight minutes to play, a good, solid win, building on the game at Charlestown. Manny had scored twenty-six points, and it was as though everything else fed off him, the game getting easier for everyone.

"I'm going to yell at you," Nyblom said a few minutes later in the Health Room to Clements, "and I'm going to yell at him."

He pointed to Manny.

"And I'm going to yell at him," he said, pointing to John-son Weah, "and you have to be man enough to take it."

He looked out at everyone sitting at the tables in front of him.

"Whatever you have to do academically, gentlemen, is fine," Nyblom said. "If that means you have to come late to practice because you're doing extra help, that's fine. And, gentlemen, if we play the way we can there's nobody in the state that can beat you. But you have to do it."

He paused a beat, then another.

"Wayne, you should be listening instead of talking."

• • •

One cold, sunny afternoon I sat in a Burger King in South Providence, right off I-95. I was there with Yasah Vezele, the older sister of Ben, who had been to a couple of games, one with her mother, an older woman who appeared almost stately. This, in itself, made Yasah Vezele unusual, for very few family members ever went to the games. I also had the growing suspicion that I wasn't going to be able to get a lot out of Ben. Whether it was shyness, or a certain wariness, he somehow seemed more distant than the others. He was one of the guys, no question about that, for he lived across the street from Quenton Marrow, and very close to Marquis Young and Wayne Clements, had known all three forever. Jim Black had coached his AUU team and had come to believe Ben was much more grounded than his teammates, due to his stable family situation, and that several of his AAU teammates had always seemed to gravitate to Ben because of his family.

Yasah was a decade older, attending graduate school at the University of Rhode Island. She too had been born in Liberia, going through elementary school there. Her father, who had attended college in the United States in Montana, worked for a mining company. He had fathered three girls before he married Yasah and Ben's mother.

"We went through a lot with the war and all," she said. "We thought everything was lost."

She paused.

"We've seen horrible things," she said softly.

Civil war had started in Liberia in the late '80s, and, in retrospect, it was probably inevitable. The country on the African coast had been founded by freed former American slaves, who replicated many of the same social structures they had known in the United States. But this time they were the royalty, complete with plantation-style houses. That colonization had begun in the 1820s, and in 1847 the new country became the Republic of

Liberia. Its capital city, Monrovia, was named for James Monroe, the fifth president of the United States, who had been a prominent supporter of the colonization. The descendants of these early colonists, known as America-Liberians, became the political, social, and economic leaders of the country for over 130 years, even though they were a minority of the population.

They were called the "Congo People," and in some ways they lived lavish lifestyles, with big houses, servants, trips to Europe, and vacation homes. The indigenous people were called "Country," and lived far different lifestyles: much poorer, not well educated, the servant class. But when the revolution came, led by a Liberian army sergeant named Samuel Kanyon Doe, it was brutal, with tens of thousands of civilians being massacred.

These are the broad brush strokes, but they don't tell the human story. I first became aware of what it felt like to live through that war in 1990, reading a story in the *Providence Journal* by a young black reporter named Helene Cooper, whom I used to see around the newsroom back then but didn't know. She would go on to work for both the *Washington Post* and the *New York Times*, and to publish a powerful memoir in 2008 about growing up in Liberia called *The House at Sugar Beach*.

She had written about her initial reluctance to document what she had seen as a child for fear her relatives still in Liberia would be punished, but said that she had come to believe in the power of the written word to get the story out to the world, regardless of the consequences.

"Believing that . . . ," Cooper wrote, "I wrote about what happened to my family at the hands of Doe's soldiers. I wrote about how my mother was raped at gunpoint by five drunken soldiers, in a bid to save me from a similar fate, a fate suffered by many of my ninth-grade classmates. I wrote about how my mom, my sister and I were shot at, how my father was wounded, how my uncle was executed on the beach—again by Doe's drunken soldiers. I wrote, in graphic detail, about exactly what the media was referring to when they use the phrase, 'Doe took power in a bloody pre-dawn coup.'"

The second Liberian Civil War would begin in 1997 and last six years, ending when President Charles Taylor, who once had been a student at Bentley College in Massachusetts, was eventually charged with war crimes and sent to prison. The two civil wars lasting from 1989 to 2003 killed an estimated 250,000 Liberians and displaced about a million more. The country's roads, power grid, and other basic structures were destroyed.

When Yasah Vezele was a child in Liberia there were two camps for Liberian refugees, one in Guinea and one in Ghana. Their family was Yasah, her older sister, and her parents, as Ben hadn't been born yet. Yasah was just a child. At one point her father had to pay some guides to take them out of harm's way.

"God had his hand on us," she said.

In December 1995 the family landed at Kennedy Airport in New York City, arriving with the clothes on their backs. They soon made it to Providence, which had become one of the hubs of the Liberian presence in the United States, and began to build a new life in a house in South Providence her parents built. Yasah has always seen it as a good neighborhood, one that had a lot of action in it yet never felt particularly dangerous to her, even if many of her friends no longer lived there. But she was serious about school, and she had come to believe that her schools in the Liberia of her childhood had been better than those in America. She had also come to believe that if someone had come to Hope after the tenth grade in Liberia they would have ended up the valedictorian of their class.

"My family really valued education," Yasah Vezele said. "You were expected to come home with A's. School was serious business. You were not there to fool around."

That, too, was a lesson she brought with her from Liberia, where school was something you paid to go to, something important. She had been an excellent student at Hope, and also played softball, basketball, and volleyball, in which she was the MVP for two straight years. She graduated with honors.

"I loved Hope," she said.

She then went to the University of Rhode Island, part of the school's Talent Development program, geared to help minority kids in Rhode Island with academic potential. She did very well in college, because for her college was about hard work and taking advantage of opportunities, about education and bettering yourself, all the things she calls her values.

Ben is almost a decade younger, the first boy in the family.

"He is our answered prayer," she said.

"I had to be in the house at a certain time when I was a kid," Ben told me one day. "There were rules. And education is respected."

Left unsaid was that for many of his teammates education was not respected.

Vezele also, in a certain sense, grew up with Hope in ways most of the other kids did not. His sister took him to basketball games when he was seven or eight years old. He was exposed to things as a child that many of his teammates didn't understand, maybe the most important being the value of education, its potential to change lives. But that came with a certain asterisk, too. For he knew that to get to college he was going to need a scholarship.

"I have to get a scholarship," he said. "My parents can't afford to send me to college."

This is said with no emotion, simply a statement of fact.

The team was back in the Health Room two nights later, about to play Smithfield, a suburban school in the northwest part of the state. It was a team they were expected to beat, especially after the big win over Mount Pleasant, and Nyblom was pushing the same theme he had repeated since the season began, that if they only could learn to play together and play the right way, to start thinking about the team and not just about themselves, there was no team in the state that could beat them. It had been his mantra. And if the game at Charlestown had been the turning point, the first time this team had looked like the one he had envisioned last summer, he still knew how fragile it all was. One great win against Mount Pleasant didn't mean that it would automatically transfer over to the game tonight against Smithfield. No two games were the same, and all too often his players' greatest opponents were themselves.

So when Manny came into the room eating potato chips, as casually as though he were going to take a nap somewhere, Nyblom felt a sense of foreboding.

"Who's the best shooter in the room?" one kid asked.

"I don't know," Manny said, pondering the question. "I'd say me."

"Who has the most air balls this season?" Moors asked.

"Manny," several yelled out, and everyone laughed, even Manny.

Winning did that, of course. It softened the rough edges, made everyone get along better. But Nyblom knew the team's dynamic was more complicated. So minutes later when they went out to warm up in preparation for the game, he didn't know what to expect.

Neither did Rob Whalen.

"Our body language is terrible," he said. "If you walked in here you would think someone had died. We just don't look ready. Wayne's sitting there with his shoelaces untied. Marquis is miserable because he's not playing. We just don't seem ready to play."

To make matters worse, the gym felt like a sauna. One day cold. One day hot. You never knew. The players huddled together, began their customary pregame chant:

"BLUE WAVE"

"BLUE WAVE"

"BLUE WAVE"

"OOH-AAH."

"Do you want to play today?" Nyblom asked Wayne Clements. "Because you don't look like it."

Clements shrugged.

"I'm all right."

But the team wasn't. By halftime they were back in the Health Room and down two.

"This is awful," Jim Black said softly as we walked into the room together.

Nyblom certainly thought so.

"You let this team, this team that's much less athletic than you are, beat you to the ball," he said. "You are three for twelve from the free-throw line. You've given them life, and if you don't come out in the second half and bury them we're going to be in trouble."

He hesitated, as if searching for the right words.

"This team is terrible, and this game is unbearable to watch. We need this game. We need this game. We need this game. Period. For if we lose this it's going to be virtually impossible to get where we're trying to go."

The second half was a struggle. Hope finally went up three with a little over nine minutes to play, and eventually ground out a nine-point win that really didn't seem like a win.

Nyblom apologized to the kids who hadn't gotten into the game, because it was becoming apparent that he was going to have a problem with Marquis Young, the nephew of Laurence Young, a junior who was not getting any meaningful time. Not only was his older brother Malieke often in the gym, but Marquis Young was a strong personality. And Nyblom knew that nothing had the potential to damage a team's delicate makeup as much as kids who didn't play a lot, especially on teams that weren't winning. This had been a game when he figured he had a chance to get everyone some significant minutes, the kind of game that keeps teams happy, the reward for all the tough practices, a continuation of the trip to Charlestown. But it hadn't happened, as if the trip to Charlestown and the good feeling of that day had been an aberration and now they were back in the same holding pattern they had been in since practice had first started.

So now he pointed to Wayne Clements.

"This little mutt, who stunk in the first half, made a big shot and played great in the second half. But, gentlemen, there's no excuse not to have beaten that team by twenty-five tonight. But my wife's in the gym and she brought some cookies, so let's go celebrate.

"But one more thing.

"You have two weeks before the semester ends, and if you have any problem in class, or at home, or with one of your teachers and you need a place to get away for a while, you can come stay with me and we'll get something worked out. And remember, when you show up late teachers come to me. And when you're acting silly, Jeremy, they also come to me. All right, let's come together."

"ONE, TWO, THREE, HOPE," they all yelled as they gathered in a circle.

But the next afternoon at practice, once again, it was like starting from scratch. Manny wasn't there. Delonce Wright had left school sick. Wayne was wearing a yellow practice jersey, while everyone else was in blue-and-white ones, and a sophomore kid from the jayvee team named J.J. was there. Or LBH, as Moors referred to him.

"Lucky to Be Here," Moors said. "Every year we have one. Just like we have an 'All World' every year."

"You guys can screw up an easy practice," bellowed Nyblom.

A few minutes later Manny walked in.

"Where you been?" Nyblom asked.

"I had to do something for my aunt."

Nyblom just shook his head and walked way. But a few minutes later, after witnessing another basketball mini-atrocity, a graphic reminder of why they were 3-5 and staring up from a deep hole if they wanted to make the playoffs, he yelled out, "CAN WE PLEASE PAY ATTENTION?"

"Wayne doesn't remember any of the three years he's been here," muttered Moors. "The teams he's played against. Any of it."

But Dennis Wilson is back from whatever hiatus he's been on, or as Johnson Weah said to Moors, after being asked where Wilson had been, "This is Hope; we have things to do."

"Hey, Johnson, want some fried goat tomorrow?" Moors shot back, a reference to Johnson's Liberian childhood.

Johnson laughed.

It was all low key, a reminder that the season was a long, emotional journey. Long ago Nyblom had learned that it can't be all out, every day. He had also learned that his players' emotional state was infinitely more important than their physical one.

The next day wasn't low key.

It was Saturday, January 12, and Hope had another non-league game scheduled, against East Hartford, a Connecticut high school. All the players were there except Jeremy Rivera, a small reserve guard, who rarely played.

"Jeremy's all done," Nyblom said with no emotion in his voice. "Angel said he'd rather work."

Jeremy had also quit last year, but had played in the fall league, asking for another chance. Now he was gone again.

East Hartford was another inner-city team, save for one little white point guard no one from Hope could defend, who played like a pint-sized version of NBA star Steve Nash, darting here, there, and everywhere, even as he played with a long gray shirt underneath his uniform top. It was a decent game, played before a smattering of people, Hope eventually losing 73-60.

Both teams gathered afterward in the cafeteria, a large room in the school's basement, maybe thirty yards from where the boys' locker room was. It was an old, drab room with red and white pillars and a big yellow sign on the wall that said, "Show Your Politeness, Respect, Discipline, Excellence."

There were trays of food, served by Nyblom's wife, Tammie, and his mother, Audrey; Nyblom not only loved to cook, he spent part of his summers working for a caterer, and often brought meals to his players. But the highlight of the afternoon was an impromptu "rap-off" between the two teams. They stood next to each other in the cafeteria, with one kid from East Hartford rapping, then one from Hope. Rap as theater. Rap as competition. Rap as sport. Rap as verbal shorthand. Rap as one of the lifebloods of these kids' world; the music that sprang from the same inner-city neighborhoods they were growing up in, the music that not only spoke to their experience of the word, but glorified it, too—the street violence, the misogyny, the attitude, all of it. It's the music that had long ago defined youth culture, and it was now everywhere, from the halftime shows at the Super Bowl, to its biggest stars being invited to the White House, deeply imbedded in American culture.

The two teams went back and forth, in each other's faces, more animated than they had been during the game, for this was competition too, and maybe more important because it was theirs and theirs alone. No coaches. No schools. No referees in striped shirts. No adults imposing their rules and regulations, their structure.

Until the final rap.

"I know you're totally hip to your fade," one of the Hartford players rapped, his teammates right behind him, the Hope players right in front of him, all the kids energized, "but that one looks like it's homemade."

He then fell back into the arms of his cheering teammates, who caught him as though he had just hit a dramatic walk-off home run and they were meeting him at home plate in triumph and about to carry him off in some symbolic chariot, as if Hope had lost both the game and the rap contest, too.

CHAPTER NINE

You couldn't spend any time at practice without becoming aware of the alumni, the ones who drifted in and out. Whether it was Shaquille Jones, or Malieke Young, or someone else, each one of them had a story.

On this day it was Shaun Hill.

It was a name I remembered, even if I couldn't remember seeing him play in high school. But he had been All State for two years less than a decade ago, another local comet who had disappeared just as fast, one more sad reminder of the old Jimmy Breslin line that "ghetto stars burn out quickly." He had gone to the Community College of Rhode Island, a junior college about fifteen minutes south of Providence in Warwick, but he had lasted only a couple of weeks. Now he was just another young black male who was looking for something, no easy thing in a state where the unemployment rate for young black males is 40 percent.

He had grown up with a mother who struggled with addiction issues, and never knew who his father was until he had all but grown up. Hill had been thrown out of Roger Williams Middle School for what he says was "ruthfulness," and grew up in South Providence's dystopian world of guns, fights, and violence. He was nine years old when he watched his grandfather die after being shot on Public Street.

"I refuse to be a statistic," he said. "Nyblom's like my father. I tell kids all the time—do the right thing and he will do anything for you."

"That's Dave's new project," Moors said. "Trying to get him into school somewhere. He's a good player. Then again, we've had guys who have been out of school twenty years and come back and dominate our guys."

He pointed over to the corner where Wayne Clements was lying in the bleachers with an ice pack on his knee.

"Wayne's still getting dressed," he said. "We've been practicing an hour."

"Let's go," Nyblom said, frustration in his voice. "We've got La Salle tomorrow and if we get drilled just remember this practice. Wayne, if you don't want to be here go home. Hey, fellas, have we won ten in a row? Am I missing something here? Are we the favorite to win the state tournament? Because this effort stinks."

Wayne had come late because he'd had tutoring after school, had gone through two drills and now said his knee hurt.

"Yo, Wayne, get in the game," said Manny. "I want to bang on you."

"Hey, Wayne, get in the game," said Ben. "I want to dunk on you."

Wayne didn't respond to them. He was on his cell phone.

"I can't," he said into his phone. "I'm at practice."

A few minutes later Malieke Young got into the scrimmage. He doesn't remember his father, who is in jail, but he and his brother Marquis have different fathers. In many ways Laurence

Young, their uncle, had been their surrogate father; he was the one who had made it, the one who had followed the bouncing ball out of the neighborhood to Rider in New Jersey, then on to professional basketball in Brazil. Malieke had gone to Hope because his uncle had gone to Hope. He and Laurence Young were very close; his uncle had brought Malieke to New Jersey one summer so he could play on a Jersey AAU team, and Laurence had told Malieke he was like a son to him. Malieke could cry in front of his uncle, could be vulnerable in ways he couldn't be with anyone else. He was at Wayne's house when he first heard that Laurence Young had died, and the hurt went through him like a knife to the heart.

Laurence Young used to ride his bike from South Providence to Hope so he could get in extra workouts; he could have gone either way and he went the right way, became the embodiment of Nyblom's vision.

So now Malieke Young, seven months out of high school, and with no real place to go, was in the practice because Hope needed bodies.

"Basketball is my life," he said.

But in all the important ways he was already about the past, or at least it seemed that way on this afternoon in this old gym. For the sad, irrefutable reality about high school basketball is that it's over in the blink of an eye, that there are always kids coming behind you pushing you out. Even if you're not ready to go.

This practice session was just one more example, for there was always another game to prepare for, another game to play.

Afterward, the players sat on the floor at center court.

Nyblom stood over them in his blue sweatshirt and tan shorts.

"Useless today," he said, pointing at Wayne.

"Useless today," he said, pointing at Devante Youn.

"Mostly useless today," he said pointing at Manny and Johnson Weah.

"Half useless today," he said to Delonce Wright.

On and on it went, a mostly useless day.

"This is reality," said Bob Whalen, assistant coach Rob Whalen's father, and maybe Hope's biggest fan. He was there at all the games, always sitting close to the Hope bench. "A Catholic school and an inner-city school."

Yes, it was.

This divide had long defined the Rhode Island Interscholastic League, and rarely without a certain controversy, even if it's often understated. Because the state is so small, the parochial schools and the public schools play in the same league, even though the Catholic schools have always enjoyed certain advantages, namely that they can attract kids from around the state and not just from a certain geographic area. They also have a long history of athletic success, whether it's Mount St. Charles hockey, which has dominated the state for decades, or traditional all-sports powers Hendricken and La Salle.

So there's always been a certain resentment, however couched, complete with rumors of illegal recruiting, and the fatalistic attitude that this is just the way it is. It had only increased in recent years as both Hendricken and La Salle have been recruiting more black kids, many of whom would be in inner-city schools if they had stayed in public school, in an attempt to make their school populations more diverse.

La Salle was founded in downtown Providence in 1871 as an all-male school established by the Christian Brothers, a Roman Catholic teaching order. By 1925 it had outgrown its original building and moved into a neighborhood in the northwest corner of the city called Elmhurst, just a couple of blocks away from Providence College. It has long been an institution in Rhode Island, with an alumni list of various political and civic leaders, including U.S. senator Jack Reed. LaSalle had transformed itself in recent years, from a traditional all-boys school in one red-brick building that spoke of another time to a co-ed school with a new arts building, a new field house, and new athletic fields in back, to the point that it looked like a suburban school.

Pictures of the past lined the hallway that led to the visiting locker room inside the field house. The hallway was carpeted. There was a donor's wing. The locker room was clean and well lit, with maroon lockers and white cinder-block walls. It all seemed new. Not like Hope, where pieces of old gum were stuck to the worn gray stairs leading up to the gym.

One little slice of irony was that three of the La Salle players were East Side kids, specifically Camp Street kids—Dexter Thomson, Keon Wilson, and Mikey Clark. There also was the feeling that La Salle was looking to cherry-pick the best football players from the Mount Hope Cowboys, one of the top youth football teams in the state, one that relied heavily on East Side kids and was run by Lorenzo Perry, a former great football player at La Salle who had grown up in the same area.

"Dexter would love to be here with us," Nyblom said. "He's always in our gym. But I'm never going to put pressure on a kid."

Hope's rivalry with La Salle had become personal in ways that other rivalries hadn't. Some of that, undoubtedly, was spillover from the fall league, when there had been a little skirmish in one of the games between Hope and La Salle, specifically between Delonce Wright and Jared Thompson, a white guard from La Salle. Then there was the fact that Hope had upset La Salle in the quarterfinals of the state tournament last year.

"These guys got beat by twenty last time," Nyblom said to his team in the locker room, "so they're going to be coming after you."

As soon as the team went out to warm up the jayvee team came slinking in, Pedro Correia behind them, rolling his eyes. They had lost by forty, and sometimes you wondered if they had ever played organized basketball before, so helter-skelter they were, so outclassed in so many of their games.

"Whatever's not yours, don't take it," Nyblom said to them forcefully.

Outside in the cavernous field house maroon banners were on the walls, nine state championship banners in girls' soccer since 2001. There were roughly 250 people in the bleachers. There was a public address system. There were cheerleaders in maroon-and-white uniforms. This was an atmosphere you rarely found at the Hope home games.

La Salle started out in a zone defense, and right away Hope was in trouble, as if a basic zone defense were some new mathematical equation and they hadn't done their homework. By halftime they were down thirteen, had thrown the ball away fourteen times, and Nyblom was red-faced and angry.

"If we can't play together we have no chance to win," he said emphatically. "That team is out-executing you, and they are out-working you. They get layup after layup because they keep beating you down the court."

He stopped for a breath.

"Energy and effort. It's desire, gentlemen. They are out-working you in every aspect of the game."

He paused again, and when he spoke again his voice was lower.

"We can't make you do it, fellas, but if you keep playing like this there won't be any divisional playoffs, never mind the big dance. There won't be anything."

"The problem is you all know these guys," Moors said. "You're all friends, and you're too nice."

With just under twelve minutes to play Hope was only down

three, back in the game. They had come out in the second half with much more intensity, and their level of play instantly rose. Then Angel Rivera was subbed in for Wayne Clements as La Salle was about to shoot a foul shot. Instead of coming directly over to the Hope bench Wayne walked over to the opposite side of the court and toward the other end of the gym.

"WAYNE," yelled out Nyblom, motioning him to walk across the court and come to the bench. Wayne ignored him and kept walking.

He walked all the way to the far baseline as Nyblom stared at him. Wayne slowly walked across the baseline, then came over and sat at the far end of the Hope bench, as far away from the coaches as he could get, three seats removed from the closest Hope player.

A few minutes later, as the game continued, a handful of high school kids sitting five rows behind the bench began chanting, "WE WANT WAYNE."

They did it three times before Wayne turned around and ran his hand across his throat, his way of telling them to knock it off.

A few minutes later Hope was down thirteen, the game starting to get away from them. Nyblom called a time out. Wayne stood on the outside of the huddle, and when the time out was over he walked back to the far end of the bench. With just two minutes left to play Manny hit a three-pointer, and Hope was down seven with momentum on their side, having put together a frantic couple of minutes. It had been a nice little comeback, bringing some excitement back to the game. But in the end they were done in by their past transgressions, all those old sins that kept showing up like kids crashing a party.

Once again Hope was in a losing locker room, their league record a dismal 3-6.

And Nyblom was pointing at Wayne.

"You guys have to talk to him," he said, addressing the team. "He's selfish and he hangs his head the minute things don't go well. But he won't listen to me and he won't listen to the other coaches. Maybe he'll listen to you."

The room was quiet. Manny sat by himself in one corner, saying nothing. Wayne had his head down, not looking at anyone.

"You sulked," Nyblom said, looking at him.

Then he addressed the boys sitting on the benches in front of him.

"It's the halfway part of the season and we're 3-6. This guy wants to be the leading scorer. This guy wants to make All Division. This guy's pissed off because he doesn't play enough. This guy's pissed because he doesn't get enough shots. This guy's pissed because he's always pissed. There's simply too much selfishness on this team. You let one get away tonight. This can't keep going on, gentlemen."

Wayne didn't look up.

Into the room walked Arondae Washington, a rugged black man who had once been a very good player at Hope; he was the father of two La Salle players, Keon Wilson and Mikey Clark. Once upon a time, back when he had been at Hope, he had run through the streets of Alexandria, Virginia, with Bill Clinton, when the former president had been involved in the Institute for International Sport, a Rhode Island–based organization. Washington had been picked to run with Clinton, and when he was told that he was going to run with the former president he thought someone was fooling around. And while he was running he kept smiling, to the point that Clinton asked, "Why do you keep smiling?"

"Because you're in front of me," Washington told him.

He had been a senior on Nyblom's first team, back in 1996.

"I'm still a Hope guy," he said to Nyblom.

"You used to be a Hope guy," Nyblom said.

Later, Washington would say, "They're all like my sons," referring to the players in the game, "for I know where they come from."

The players were starting to drift out of the room. Because the game had been on the west side of the city there was no reason to go back to Hope on the East Side, where none of them lived anyway. One of the last left in the locker room was Devante Youn, a big kid with a shy smile. He never said much, and because he had gone to Fatima, a Catholic school south of the city, attending for a year before being unable to afford it, and since he now went to E-Cubed during the day, he was a little bit of an outlier on the Hope team. He wasn't part of the so-called Five Bros, as Marquis, Aaron, Eli, Quenton, and Ben liked to call themselves, as they all lived close to each other in South Providence. He wasn't a senior, like Manny, Delonce, Wayne, and Johnson. He didn't have an outgoing personality like Angel. But he had a big strong body and a few decent moves around the basket, and Nyblom was forever on him for not being in good enough shape, for not working hard enough. He never said much, had a certain reserved manner about him that many of the others didn't possess.

I knew he lived somewhere in the vicinity, and asked him if he needed a ride. The only time I had ever dealt with him was when Jim Black, the third volunteer assistant coach, was helping him with his foul shooting one day after practice. He was having trouble, his form too erratic, and I too was trying to give him a little advice.

"Follow through, Devante," I told him. "Put your hand right in the basket."

He kept missing.

"Devante," I finally said, exasperated. "Make three in a row and I'll give you twenty bucks."

I figured there was no way in the world he was going to make three foul shots in a row. And, of course, he did. And, of course, I had to give him the twenty. And, of course, he laughed.

So that was our history, thin as it was.

He lived in a small house on the other side of Providence College, almost in North Providence, with his mother, stepfather, and older sister. His parents had come from Liberia, and when he first started going to school in Providence he couldn't believe how so many of the other kids in kindergarten were screaming and acting out all the time. So he had ended up in Catholic schools, and when he began high school at Fatima, in a town fifteen miles south of Providence, he had needed to wake up at 4:30 in the morning, put on a uniform, and get to the bus stop; he slept the entire ride. Fatima was only about 5 percent African American, so he was always different. The basketball team was horrible, and it was never easy being there, the long days being just a part of the challenge. Fatima was different from the Providence schools; kids didn't talk back to the teachers and act out, and the environment was helping him as a student. He did homework, he earned A's and B's and was an honor student. And even though his family could no longer afford to send him there, he knew that in many ways Fatima had served him well.

If nothing else, it made him a serious student, to the point that even though he loved basketball he knew that his education was far more important, and that his education, not basketball, would take him places in life. So now he was an honor roll student, wanted to be a civil engineer someday. He had heard so much about Liberia from his mother, how beautiful it was before the war came and changed everything, and he thought he might want to go back there someday and help out. But for now he liked E-Cubed, and he was doing his homework and taking school seriously.

"So you're smart?" I asked.

He smiled.

"I'm trying to be," he said.

But too many kids weren't trying to be smart. Or if they were, they weren't succeeding. At least not according to the standardized tests.

Tests had become the national education story, the attempt to find out what was really going on inside America's classrooms. Whether it was "Race to the Top" or "No Child Left Behind" or the latest popular slogan of the year, public education in the United States had become a huge political football, especially in American cities. That was certainly the case in Rhode Island, where the NECAP—a standardized test designed to measure student achievement—was highly controversial.

In mid-December, three weeks into the Hope basketball season, a woman named Carole Marshall wrote an op-ed piece in the *Providence Journal*, Rhode Island's only statewide newspaper.

She wrote that she had left Hope the previous June, after almost two decades of teaching in the Providence public schools. She had been one of the key figures when Hope had been broken down into three smaller learning communities, a decision that saw test scores rise; in 2002, she noted, the New England Association of Schools and Colleges took Hope off the warning list and accredited it, making Hope the only school in the city besides Classical to be accredited. She also wrote that in 2009 two thirds of the junior class in two of the three small learning communities achieved proficiency in reading.

But that progress began to change five years ago, as "all activity was subsumed under the massive burden of standardized testing and record-keeping."

She wrote that the tests were completely unrelated to the curriculum and did not recognize the various challenges facing urban populations, and that when the results came back the students "were harangued in grade-wide assemblies with threats of not being able to graduate."

"Shamefully," she continued, "we have engineered segregated schools for our urban youth and deprived them of equal resources for education."

By chance one afternoon, I ran into an old pickup basketball friend who now teaches at Hope.

"I've been in the system twenty years, three here," he said. "I got kids who show up for class without a notebook. What's up with that? Classical is the only school in the city with stability. Here we have a curriculum we follow and that's it. But I have way too many kids, and they come and go so much my head is spinning. 'Fuck' is a common word, and the amount of vulgarity is staggering. It's common speech.

"The other day I'm walking down a corridor and there are three kids standing there. I look over to see if I know one of them, and one kid says, 'What the fuck you looking at?' So I took the kid around the corner and said, 'You can't talk to people like that,' and he just stared at me like he had no idea what I was talking about.

"But it's always been crazy. I started at Roger Williams Middle School in South Providence and that was like the Wild West, even back then. So this really is nothing new. A kid raises his hand, says he has to go to the bathroom, and comes back in an hour. And they're evaluating teachers? It's their fault? It's like a two-car accident and the cop comes to investigate and he turns to the bystander and says, 'It's your fault.'

"But the sad thing, the really sad thing? We're talking about real people here."

CHAPTER TEN

Two days after the fiasco at La Salle, and one day after a waste of a practice, Manny walked into the gym.

"ALL WORLD," Keith Moors yelled out.

Manny laughed and shook his head.

"Yesterday was a waste. We only had eight guys. We had guys in Credit Recovery," Moors said, referring to the program where academic credits can be made up. "Some guys didn't come to school. Then we had a kid show up who's a 'safety transfer' from Mount Pleasant."

"What's a safety transfer?" I asked.

"That's when someone's life's been threatened," he said.

Oh.

Hope would face St. Raphael Academy of Pawtucket at home the next game, another so-called must game in a season that was coming down to a lot of "must games" if they were going to get into the playoffs.

"My fault," said Ben Vezele after he made a bad pass.

Nyblom stopped practice.

"What did you say, Ben? 'My fault'? That might be a first. No one ever says 'my fault' around here."

Then again, Ben Vezele is different from many of his teammates. And it's more than just the fact that he has two parents living in the same house with him, although on this team that makes him unique. He grew up different from many of his friends, even those who lived in the same neighborhood, down near where Prairie Avenue runs into Thurber's Avenue in South Providence. He'd always had a curfew, for one thing. His family had its own house for another. He was also expected to be a good student, to take school seriously. For in his family education was seen as the passport to a better life. These were the values he'd come of age with, values that were unquestioned in his family.

In many ways it was another hybrid practice. Delonce and Johnson were on a recruiting trip to Western Connecticut College for football. Malieke Young and Shaun Hill, two of the alumni, were practicing because the team needed bodies. At one point the team engaged in a shooting drill, with what seemed like one miss after another.

"BRICK CITY!" yelled out Moors. "My daughter's eighth-grade Coventry team shoots better than this."

But if Hope wanted to make the playoffs, the situation was critical. They needed to win games. So by the time they'd assembled the next day in the Health Room directly after school for a pregame meeting, the game still four hours away, there was a certain sense of urgency. At least for Nyblom.

"We're waiting on Wayne," he said.

"Where he at?" came a voice.

"That's what I'm asking you."

"Where's Khalil?"

"Khalil's done," Nyblom said.

So was the transfer from Mount Pleasant. He had lasted one day.

"We're here for you, gentlemen," he said. "Home problems. Girlfriend problems. School problems. Whatever it is."

It was a constant message, one that said that underneath all the tough love and all the emotion and pressure of a season, these players could ask the coaches for help. Some understood it. Some didn't. But you couldn't spend any time in the Hope gym without the sense that there was a basketball family at Hope, however dysfunctional it could seem. It was the delicate terrain Nyblom was always walking on—demanding and hard-edged one day, bringing food and telling kids they could use his house as a sanctuary the next.

A few minutes later most of the players left, but to where? It was now just three hours before the game, certainly not enough time to go home and come back again, not when none of them had a car. Some might have been walking down Olney Street to University Heights, a small shopping center that had a Mc-Donald's. But that required money. Most of them were merely hanging around in the small gym that was next to the main gym playing an inner-city game called Knockout, where one guy has the ball and calls for someone else to come out and guard him while everyone else stands around and watches, a game they play in their street clothes, a game that seemed to have little to do with basketball and everything to do with socializing.

Except for Manny.

He stayed in the Health Room on the one computer in the room for a few minutes before we began to talk.

He was saying how he used to practice speaking into a mirror, and how he first started playing basketball to keep him out of trouble, a new kid in this strange land. That was the beginning of his career, and soon it evolved into traveling around the city to find better competition. And soon basketball became one of his teachers too, for it was where he learned to treat people the way he wanted to be treated, the game as acceptance, the game as validation, the game as a potential ticket to a world he knew only from television.

And maybe most of all?

"Basketball gave me good friends," he said.

"Where are you going to eat before the game?" I asked.

He looked as though the question had come out of a different world.

"I'm not going to eat."

"What, you don't have any money in your pocket?"

"I never have any money," he said matter-of-factly.

"So you're going to play a game tonight when you haven't had anything to eat since noon?"

He shrugged.

"Maybe somebody will give me a candy bar," he said.

Before the game a team picture was taken, one of those that will end up in either a yearbook or maybe on a wall someday, one of those generic team pictures that captured a certain moment in time. It was taken at the foul line, the players in their blue uniforms with gold trim, the coaches in their blue shirts and tan slacks, Rob Whalen and Keith Moors on the left, Jim Black and Dave Nyblom on the right.

The picture will show the players as high school kids, their youth and their smiling faces captured forever. It will never show that it was taken on a cold winter night just minutes before they were going to play a vital game in a season that never had seemed to get started and now was slipping away. It will never show that Manny was hungry and Wayne was unhappy and both Delonce and Johnson were up in the air as to where they were going to be next year, these two high school football stars who had been instrumental in getting Hope into a playoff game in the fall, and for whom next year was a blank slate just a few months away.

Hope's fear was a very talented little St. Ray's guard named Charles Correa, arguably as talented a player as there was in the Interscholastic League, even if he was only five-foot-eight on a good day. But he was very strong, extremely quick, had great shooting range, and in Rhode Island high school basketball circles everyone knew who Charles was. Two years before, St. Ray's had won the state title, but now their games often seemed like Charles against the world and too often the world was winning and St. Ray's was just another struggling team chasing the playoffs.

They were guided by Tom Sorrentine, a veteran coach with long gray hair who looked like he was headed to a Woodstock alumni weekend. St. Ray's is a small Catholic school in nearby Pawtucket, located in the virtual shadow of McCoy Stadium, where the Red Sox's Triple-A franchise plays. Sorrentine had been coaching for decades now; he was a Rhode Island coaching institution—in the middle of a tough season.

St. Ray's troubles would continue as Hope jumped off to a 20-6 lead and never really looked back, eventually winning by nineteen points. But even after a win, there always seemed to be issues to deal with. Who was pouting because he didn't think he'd played enough? Who seemed down, for whatever the reason?

"I know you're pissed, Angel," Nyblom said afterward. "It's nothing you did wrong. So let's not ruin it by hanging heads."

Angel sat in the corner of the locker room with a forlorn look on his face.

"Again, Angel, it's nothing you did wrong."

You couldn't dislike Angel, for he had a smile that could break hearts. A couple of weeks earlier, when he was upset over a lack of playing time after a game Hope had won, his pout all over his face, I had pulled him into a corner of the locker room.

"Were you ever in a play, Angel?" I asked.

"What do you mean?"

"Were you ever in a school play when you were a little kid?"

"Yeah," he said. "Once in a while."

"Well, that's what you've got to do now," I said to him. "You've got to pretend you're not pissed. You've got to act. You don't have to like it, but you can't let the coaches see that. Especially after you win. You have to act happy, even if you have to fake it."

Angel often seemed to be a prisoner of his pride, the result of both his small size and maybe the fact that he was the only player of Puerto Rican heritage on the team. There was little question he was an overachiever on the court. Kids who are five-foot-eight in today's basketball world must play above their stature. He was also trying to be more receptive to what coaches called coaching, and what kids too often perceived as criticism. This was the delicate balancing act, especially with kids who didn't have strong father figures in their lives, kids who often perceived criticism as attacks on their manhood. It was the fine line Nyblom and the other coaches walked, trying to get their players to view coaching as constructive, not denigrating. But Angel was better now at dealing with coaching than he had been when the season started.

"I listen to the coaches more," he said one day, "instead of talking back. I used to think I was always right. I'm trying to be better with that. Because every time I had an attitude it took me away from my game."

In many ways he had come to basketball late, already fourteen when he started taking the game seriously. Before that he was never really into sports, but he played on a Boys & Girls Club team in Chad Brown and got hooked. In the eighth grade he moved back to Puerto Rico for a year, even though at the time he didn't really know Spanish, so it turned out to be a lost year academically.

But, to him, basketball is more important than school.

"I don't do homework," he said. "I'm too tired."

He paused.

"This year I have bad grades."

"Why?" I asked.

"I cut a lot of classes. It's boring. Then I have English after lunch and I always fall asleep. Some of the books I liked, but most of them I just found boring."

He paused again.

"A lot of kids cut classes. I don't think anybody does homework. But I'll stay after school every once in a while and do my work."

Since Chad Brown, the housing project where he lives, is very close to Providence College he feels he has a certain knowledge of college life, one gleaned from observation more than anything else.

"There are a lot of parties there," said Angel Rivera. "That's what you want to do in college."

It was a Monday, Martin Luther King, Jr. Day.

There was no school.

But there was practice.

One of the players was taking off his coat, getting down to his baggy white shorts and long blue shirt.

"What did Martin Luther King do?" I asked.

The kid looked at me a beat too long.

"Free the slaves?"

"No," I said. "A president did that. Do you know his name?"

"Abraham," he said.

"That's the first name. What's the second?"

He looked at me for another beat too long.

"Abraham," he said, before walking away.

Hope would come back three nights later and beat East Providence at home to make their record 5-6. More important, they had now won two straight games for only the second time all year, and so when they came into the gym it was with a certain swagger, one that created the best practice in a long time, one without sulking, without pouting, and the sense that this was an improving team.

Was it finally going to be different now?

"We go through this every year," Moors said, shaking his head.

There was no question Manny was better, happier, more engaged with his teammates, to the point that Nyblom thought he was finally coming around.

"These kids have to get out of Providence," Moors said, as he watched the end of practice. "It's a big growing-up thing. They can't come running home to their friends and keep doing the same stupid stuff they're always doing. They have to get away and figure it out. New friends. New people."

He had done that, going off to Mount Ida Junior College outside of Boston after he graduated from Tolman High School in neighboring Pawtucket. After two years he had parlayed that into playing basketball at Eastern Connecticut, and even if that had not exactly worked out, in the end it had no doubt broadened his world, no insignificant thing for someone who had spent some of his adolescence in a group home.

"These kids are always fighting the stereotypes," he continued. "They're thugs. They're doing drugs. They'll never get out of the ghetto. They're street. They're going to rob you, beat you up. That's what these kids hear all the time.

"And do you know what I hear all the time? Why do you

coach them? Why do you waste your time on them? That's why I don't mind being the bad cop. Because I know what these kids face, because I went through a lot of it myself. And it's worse now. So I need to be the bad cop."

To him it was simple: Hope, and the kids who went to it, needed more structure.

"If I were running things here there would be uniforms in school," he said. "No pants hanging down around your ass. No cell phones. No talking back to teachers. No walking out during the day. None of the foolishness you see all around here. It would be like an academic boot camp."

Moors had come to learn a lot of things in his six years coaching at Hope. He knew that things are always easier in the summer league, but then school starts and the distractions start too. And that you had to cultivate patience, because you never knew what was going on at home with kids, even if you thought you did. And the most important thing he had learned?

"You're not going to save them all," Moors said. "We start with twenty and we end up with twelve. Every year we have setbacks. That's what happens. Every year."

CHAPTER ELEVEN

Classical is the academic star of the Providence public school system and always has been. In 2012 *Newsweek* called it one of the country's best high schools. Ninety-five percent of its graduates go on to college. It's the alma mater of American humorist S. J. Perelman, former U.S. senator John O. Pastore, two former Rhode Island governors, columnist Joe Nocera of the *New York Times*, and the *Times*'s movie critic A. O. Scott.

It was founded in 1843, and since 1970 has been at its present location at the border of South Providence and the West End, cut off from downtown by I-95. It's also a building in the Brutalist tradition, big and tan stone and unappealing, like a state building in a dreary eastern European country.

"It's no wonder Modernism has gotten such a bad reputation in Rhode Island," one guide to Providence architecture says.

For Delonce Wright it was practically a home game. He lived in an apartment just a few blocks away, on a side street near a reputed drug house, one of those places the police have raided innumerable times through the years. His father had been away in the military most of his life, and he's sometimes gone three or four years without seeing him, but he said that didn't bother him, and "it's no excuse for me." He is the oldest of three, and lived in several different places around the city when he was younger. For a while it was Manton Heights, a housing project in the West End, the same one Manny had lived in when he first came to Providence. Later, it was Chad Brown, where Angel Rivera now lived. Delonce was about eight, but even then he knew it was a dangerous place.

"I didn't go outside much then," he said, "because there were shootings and stuff. I probably heard twenty gunfights. But it teaches you how to stay safe. To choose wisely. Your friends. People you bring to your house. I have a relative who was in and out of jail, and one serving life for murder. You learn that anything can happen at any time, and you have to be prepared for anything."

This was said dispassionately, as though he were talking about all the summer camps he'd been to, and the people he met there.

"I think I'm pretty responsible," he continued, "because I've seen the kids who have dropped out of school. They do nothing. Absolutely nothing. And I don't want to be like them."

He was a senior, but his educational journey had been complicated. As a young kid he went to the Paul Cuffee School, Providence charter school, sent there by his mother, who went to Hope and then to the University of Rhode Island. In ninth grade he was a day student at St. Andrew's, a prep school in Barrington, a tony suburb ten miles south of Providence, sent there because one of the people who works at Paul Cuffee is on the board at St. Andrew's. He was one of only about twenty black kids in the school, and when it didn't work out at St. Andrew's he went to Hope because he knew some kids there. So, in a sense, he was a little different from most of his teammates, for he'd been exposed to more, even if he was from the same inner-city neighborhoods.

"I was upset when I was thrown out of St. Andrew's," he said. "Hope was big and loud and noisy compared to Paul Cuffee and St. Andrew's, and it was much easier. I've never felt it's challenging. There have been times in class with the work where I've said to myself, 'I've seen this before.' But I liked the teachers right away. They acted like they cared. But I thought it was too free. You could walk right out the front door and nothing was going to happen to you. It was very different from St. Andrew's. The classes were bigger and the way they were taught was different too."

The other main difference was that at Hope was there always seemed to be a handful of kids who distracted the teachers, distracted everybody.

Delonce had played football since he was a little kid, when he was on a team called the North End Raiders. This past summer he went to a football camp at Boston College, where he ran a 4.4 in the forty-yard dash, a time that makes football people look at their stopwatch twice. He was put in a special group after that, and in the fall received some interest from several small-college football schools, Salve Regina in Newport, Rhode Island, being one of them.

"Football changed my life," he said. "It was my motivation to come to school."

He had known both Wayne Clements and Malieke Young since he was a young kid at the Sackett Street rec center, where Wayne's father was the director. He first knew Johnson Weah when they both played for Team Providence before they went to Hope. But he was now closest to Manny. He also knew many of the kids he was playing against, because to him the league was full of "street people," the inner-city kids he'd competed against in various youth leagues around the city.

"But losing sucks," he said. "Manny is trying to do too much. He feels pressure. Wayne feels pressure. He could always shoot, but you can see his knee is bothering him. I've known him since he's been ten. He's always been quiet. I still think we're as good as anyone. We've got a good solid eight players, but against La Salle we had no passion."

Why?

"I have no clue," he said. "I don't think teams beat us as much as we beat ourselves."

I asked him about Nyblom.

"He tries to help you in every way," he said. "That gets my respect. And if he weren't yelling, we wouldn't be listening."

That was a telling comment, because in a world full of constant noise, a frenzied world where for many inner-city kids rap music was the soundtrack to their lives, talking in hushed academic tones was almost like asking to be ignored.

A few minutes later the team sat in a large locker room at Classical. Wayne had blow-dried his hair into a retro Afro, the players had done a "BLUE WAVE COMING, we're coming at you, AH . . . AH . . . AH" chant in a circle, and now Nyblom was trying to get them focused as a loud rap song was blasting over a partition that separated the locker rooms. He looked at Wayne.

"You have to be a leader," he said.

He turned around.

"Coach Moors? You got anything to say?"

"Four-and-six," Moors said. "That's all you'll hear from me. Four-and-six. That's it."

It was a good game. Classical had three talented players, even if they were all smaller than six-foot-one. The best one was Kealen Ives, who had grown up with several of the Hope kids. He was only five-foot eight, but lightning quick, and a very good three-point shooter. You would have thought you were in an inner-city high school, for most of the team, the cheerleaders, and the crowd that sat in bleachers located on one side of the court were nonwhite. One of them was Buster Clements, Wayne's father.

I had a certain connection with him, as loose as it was. He once had played at St. Andrew's for Mike Raffa, a childhood friend of mine, and had been one of the first black players at St. Andrew's. He had been sent there by a man named Emil John, who used to work nights on the sports desk of the *Providence Journal* and spent his days and weekends as the minister of the Trinity Methodist Church off Broad Street in South Providence. Emil John was a big, quiet man who always wore a dark eye shade at work, and he had gone to Brown, where he had been a basketball teammate of Joe Paterno. One of his many functions at the church was coaching the youth basketball team, and one of his prized players forty years ago had been Buster Clements.

Hope was down three at the half, Nyblom telling them in the locker they were too "geeked up," and had to "slow down mentally, not physically." With a little over two minutes to play they were only down two in a seesaw of a game, until Manny was called for an offensive foul with just thirty-eight seconds to play. Classical ended up winning 71-63, and once again Hope had lost a game it could have won.

Moments afterward, the players still on the court, Manny was approached by Bob Walsh, the very successful coach at Rhode Island College, a Division III school located in the northwest corner of Providence behind Mount Pleasant High School. A former assistant at Providence College, Walsh was well known locally for taking undersized inner-city kids, teaching them to play together and to play hard, and routinely turning out teams that surprised people. During the game he had also said that he liked junior Ben Vezele, whose size and potential promised that he, too, might be able to one day play in college somewhere.

But for Manny it was a visible reminder that his senior season was coming to a close, and that the start of real life was just a few short months away.

Or as Nyblom said afterward, "It's getting late, fellas."

Once again, no one went back to Hope after the game, for they now were in the part of the city where most of them lived, South Providence and the West End. It was one more consequence of the lack of neighborhood schools in Providence.

It was also just the latest example of a team seeing its season slip away, a team that had lost in the state finals the year before and had only lost two key players since then. The coaches found that so frustrating, this sense that Hope was a team that kept imploding in all the little ways, that their real opponent was themselves.

"This is what happened last year," Moors said in the gym the next afternoon as several of the kids were starting to drift in for practice. "And we're better than we were last year. That's what's driving us crazy. We're 4-7 and we don't believe it. But we had two days of bad practice and we go to La Salle and we're down twenty. They don't get it. You play like you practice, and we've had like two great practices all year."

He blew on his hands because the gym was cold again.

Now there were more kids in the gym.

"You guys are so bad you should go practice in the girls' gym and play Knockout," Moors yelled out. "That's what happens when you're 4-7. You go play Knockout in the gym with the girls."

And that was exactly where they were the next afternoon, in the little gym next door playing Knockout, along with a couple of girls. In a few hours they would play against Central, another city school, but now they were just high school kids, laughing, horsing around, no coaches, no referees, no uniforms, no fans, no pressure. Kids playing for the pure love of it. All the rest of it would come soon enough.

Downstairs in the coach's office Jim Black was on Twitter reading a tweet from Central star Jerrelle Washington.

"Going to take care of some personal business at Hope tonight, 6 o'clock," it said.

Washington, who is very friendly with Delonce Wright, is one of the top players in the state, a quick, athletic guard who spends his summers playing for the famed Boston AAU team BABC, the one that Shaquille Jones once played for. It was founded and is still run by Leo Papile, who often says he's lived in the belly of the basketball beast for over thirty years now, and who was a longtime scout for the Boston Celtics in addition to shepherding innumerable kids to college basketball.

But it's not just his involvement with BABC that makes Washington different in the insular world of Rhode Island high school basketball; it's that he spent a couple of years living in the Los Angeles area, where one of his uncles was Magic Johnson's driver. Another difference is that rhythm and blues singer Jeffrey Osborne, who grew up in Providence, and for years has sung the National Anthem at Lakers' games, is also part of his mother's extended family.

He had a big game against Hope last year in the state finals, and is the main focus in all the pregame discussion among the coaches. Central is another struggling team trying to win enough games to sneak into the playoffs, so this figured to be another close contest. None of Hope's games was easy, but this one was coming with an additional distraction, for Hope's winter dance at the casino in Roger Williams Park on the south side of the city was also scheduled for that night. That was why the game was scheduled for six o'clock instead of the usual seven, and why, Nyblom realized, his team's pregame focus, shaky in the best of

times, was not good tonight. Already there was the news that
Angel's father, who lived in Boston, had rented a car for him to
use for the dance, and that was the topic of conversation among
the players in the locker room, not the upcoming game.

"This is the team that took your state championship away
last year," Nyblom said. "I hope you remember that."

"You're 4-7," Moors added. "I hope you remember that,
too."

"You should be pissed," piped up Jim Black.

Pissed or not, Hope got off to a good start, everything going well except for Johnson Weah, who appeared to be in a funk
minutes after Nyblom took him out.

"Are you ready to play?" Nyblom asked.

Johnson shrugged.

"Are you?" Nyblom said louder.

Johnson nodded.

"I'm not the one sitting," Nyblom said, the exasperation on
his face.

In many ways Johnson Weah was the mystery man, the
hardest to read. No big surprise. He had the most tortured back
story. The refugee camp in Liberia until he was ten years old.
No school until he came to Rhode Island at the same age. His
father never in his life. His insecurity about the way he talked.
The sense that among all the players he was the one with the
most obstacles in his life. Yet there was a drive inside Johnson,
one that said that he was going to make his way in this new world
or die trying.

By halftime Hope was up twenty, and Nyblom was telling
them to step on Central's throats, then go to the dance and have
a good time.

Ah, if only things were that easy. With three and a half minutes left to play, Central was only down seven and Hope was like
a prizefighter against the ropes and starting to take a beating and

praying for the bell to ring to get him out of the round, looking nothing like the team that had played in the first half. Then
Jerrelle Washington got called for a technical foul for saying
something to a referee, banged his hand down on the scorer's
table in frustration, got another tech, and was thrown out of the
game. Over and out for Central. So now Hope was 5-7 and back
in the locker room waiting to go to the dance.

"Can we sit, gentlemen," Nyblom said as he walked into the
room.

He stood in the middle of the room, blue lockers on both
sides of him.

"Does anyone feel good about this team? You shouldn't.
After the way we played in the first half this should have been a
thirty-point win. But then everyone has to get selfish and start
doing their own thing. I can't coach you if you don't want to be
coached."

He hesitated, looked at them.

And when he spoke again his voice was soft, almost pleading.

"Please be smart tonight. Please behave. Please be smart."

CHAPTER TWELVE

They were back the next afternoon, this time at the Community College of Rhode Island about twenty minutes down I-95 in Warwick. It was another one of Nyblom's extra games against good competition, and the first thing I heard was that Angel had gotten into an accident the night before following the dance, skidding in a minor snowstorm on Route 10 at 1:30 in the morning. Eli Lewis and Aaron Lynch had been in the car with him. No one had been injured.

"They're idiots," said Wayne. "They could have been hurt." He was getting dressed in the small locker room.

"Where's Quenton?" Rob Whalen asked.

"SATs," came a voice.

"SATs?" Wayne said. "What's he smart or something?"

Also in the locker room were two kids who had just enrolled in Hope from West Virginia. They were both African American, one about six-foot-five or so, the other smaller. Did they have a Rhode Island connection? Were they eligible to play?

Were they any good? No one seemed to know anything, including Nyblom.

These kinds of games were good for Hope because they gave everyone a chance to play, especially the ones who didn't get a whole lot of time in the league games. At one point in the first half the Hope lineup was Aaron Lynch, Marquis Young, Devante Youn, Eli Lewis, and Ben Vezele, the only regular starter of the group.

"This may be the only time all season all ten guys are smiling," Nyblom said, also with a smile.

For that was the dirty little secret of all sports, regardless of the level: the ones who don't get a lot of playing time are rarely happy. And one of the Hope players who wasn't happy right now during halftime was Eli Lewis, who was on the bench while everyone else was on the court warming up, a disgusted look on his face.

"You either get up and go out there," said Nyblom, "or you sit the entire second half."

Eli continued to sit there and stare straight ahead.

Finally, without looking at Nyblom, he got up and walked onto the court.

"Oh, well," Nyblom said with a rueful smile. "That little rebellion lasted all of fifteen seconds."

They were playing Norwich Free Academy, a high school in nearby Connecticut, and if the game was another snapshot of Hope's flaws—their inconsistency being the biggest—they played well before eventually losing by six. More important, everyone had played a lot of minutes.

"What killed us?" Moors asked rhetorically. "Last night killed us. What time do you think these guys went to bed last night?"

But they were back again just two nights later in the locker room at Cranston East in their blue road uniforms with gold-and-white trim, and their assortment of different-colored socks and sneakers. Cranston borders Providence to the south, a once solidly middle-class city that now is more demographically complicated. It's a city of contrasts, with the spacious new houses of western Cranston and parts of eastern Cranston that are suburban in tone, and other parts of the city that have become Providence overflow. Forty years ago Cranston East had been one of the top hockey teams in the state; now they no longer even have a hockey team. If once you could walk through the corridors of the high school and never see a person of color, now there were three black starters and a crowd of about two hundred people that would make you think you were in a city school.

But the locker room seemed new and clean and the gym was bright and big for a Rhode Island high school. This was a huge game because Hope was simply running out of time, only four league games left after tonight.

"Our last two games we've lost two big leads and one game, gentlemen," Nyblom said.

"Who'd we lose to?" asked Devante Youn.

"Norwich Free Academy, two days ago," Nyblom said, staring at him.

"Oh, yeah," Youn said.

"And he's an A student," Wayne said, rolling his eyes.

A few kids start to stretch in the locker room, while the others were oblivious.

"We even stretch like a 5-7 team," Moors said.

The jayvee game had ended, the players standing in the hallway, many with their uniform shirts out and their shorts riding low on their hips: hip-hop basketball players.

"Someday you're going to look at pictures of yourselves with your pants falling off your butts and you won't believe how ridiculous you look," Nyblom said as he walked by them.

The National Anthem was played, the players were introduced. And for most of the first half the game was awful, rough
and chippy, both teams struggling to score. By the end of the
half Hope was leading 29-13, and Moors said to me, "We play
down to our competition."

The second half was more of the same, a rough, chaotic
game, several times coming close to getting completely out of
control. At one point Wayne was knocked to the floor on a fast-
break drive to the basket, and when the game mercifully ended
there was the sense that this had nearly become ugly.

"Just sit down," Nyblom said as everyone came into the
locker room. "Sit down and be quiet. You guys let them push
you around. You let them out-tough you."

He pointed to Ben.

"You're not freakin' tough enough, and you won't get into
the weight room and do anything about it. You could be the best
player on this team, but it's up to you."

He pointed to Johnson Weah.

"You're not ever going to get a call because you're running
your mouth to the refs."

He pointed to Eli.

"And this kid sits on the bench with his hood on, sulking."

He pointed to Marquis Young.

"With just a few seconds left you don't want to go in? That's
ignorant, with your family here to support you. If you don't want
to go in, go home. Do you want to go home?"

"That's not what I'm sayin'," Young shot back.

"TEAM, gentlemen," Nyblom said.

Four nights later they were on a yellow school bus to East Providence, a city that bordered Providence to the east, across the
Seekonk River. It was a short ride, through the East Side of Providence with its wealth and charm, then over a short bridge.

But the bus hadn't gone two blocks when Ben Vezele real-ized he had left his sneakers back at Hope. So the bus turned around and went back.

"My coach would have kept on going," muttered Moors.

On its second trip the bus went out to the front of the build-ing on Hope Street, took a quick left on Lloyd Avenue past Moses Brown, and cut through the East Side until it hit Black-stone Boulevard, arguably the most prestigious address in Prov-idence, then across the Seekonk River into East Providence.

"Ben, what are you saying?" Nyblom asked Ben, who was sitting a few rows behind him.

"Randy Moss is the best receiver ever in the NFL," Ben said.

"Ben," Nyblom countered, "you're stoned."

There was a timeless quality to these bus trips, one that cut through the generations. The coaches up front. The muffled con-versations. The sense of expectation, like soldiers going off to war. The bus dark, winter outside the windows. I had ridden on so many of them in my life, all through high school, then a year of prep school, then four years of college basketball, and in many ways they all were the same. I had always felt a mix of emotions on these rides, part anticipation, part expectation, part nerves. Pregame jitters. I had them even now. For I wanted Hope to do well. If I had started out little more than an observer, the de-tached reporter, that separation was long gone. I wanted Hope to win, because they needed to win; needed it for respect, for validation, for some tangible proof that if you worked hard enough and cared hard enough there would be some reward. It was a lesson all kids needed to learn, I realized, but maybe these kids most of all. In a certain sense it was the lesson Nyblom was always preaching in his various ways, the lesson that you can transcend your neighborhood, your family, even society's expectations for you, if you only worked hard and did the right thing.

Once, East Providence had called itself the biggest town in the United States, and its teams were still called "Townies," even if East Providence has been a city for decades. It has a big, sprawling, tan high school that had been a showplace when it first opened in the '50s but now wore its age. The gym was old, with bleachers on all four sides, but the ones behind the benches were not rolled down anymore for games. The court was old too, worn by too many kids playing on it for too many decades. This was also the place where Wayne Clements and Angel Rivera had been caught stealing a couple of basketballs last year, the reason why they were banned from entering the gym this year and were not on the bus.

"See that camera," Moors said, shaking his head, as we walked through the small hallway that led to one of the locker rooms. "Wayne and Angel took the balls right in front of the camera."

The locker room had several small individual stalls surrounded by white shower curtains, but nowhere to sit.

"This is a very big game, fellas," Nyblom said. "We need it to get to .500, but now we got two guys down. But good teams pick it up when guys don't play."

It was Senior Night at East Providence, and as part of that celebration the four Hope seniors there—Manny, Delonce, Johnson, and Aaron Lynch—were also honored, along with the East Providence seniors, the senior cheerleaders, and the parents of each. It was a reminder that East Providence was not an inner-city school, but existed in that place between the inner city and the suburbs, a place where high school sports were part of the community in ways they weren't in the Providence public schools. For decades now, East Providence drew more people to its football games than any other high school in Rhode Island, and even if tonight's attendance didn't reflect that, this was a school where sports were still important in ways they no longer were in the city schools.

East Providence was coached by Alex Butler, a light-skinned black man who had been a great player at East Providence, then at Rhode Island College, a Division III school. Once upon a time I had played high school basketball in this same gym against his father, a great athlete of his era named Junior Butler. In so many ways Rhode Island was a small place, six degrees of separation everywhere you looked.

Shortly before the game began the Hope team was again in one of their pregame circles.

"BLUE WAVE, BLUE WAVE, BLUE WAVE . . . AH, AH, AH!" they shouted.

Hope fell behind as soon as the game began, and trailed 24-21 at the half. Once again they were bothered by a zone defense, as if the very sight of one brought out all their worst basketball instincts, especially without Wayne as a point guard. Instead, they stood around too much, didn't pass the ball very well, and never seemed to make two perimeter shots in a row. It was one more reinforcement of the stereotype that inner-city kids didn't like playing against zone defenses, as if they were somehow not real basketball but rather some white version of it. A zone defense slowed Manny down and forced him to be a jump shooter—not his strength. And when Manny didn't score, all too often Hope didn't score.

The second half was another one of those close down-the-stretch games that Hope always seemed to be in, games hanging in the balance, games that could go either way. With just thirteen seconds left to play Hope was down two, the gym a madhouse, when there was a scramble for the ball. Somehow Delonce was fouled taking a three-point shot in the game's dying seconds. Not Hope's best foul shooter, but nowhere near its worst, either.

So there he was.

At the foul line with three shots.

Make them all and Hope is probably going to win.

Make two and the game is probably going to overtime.

Make just one and there still would be pressure on East Providence to score.

So he stood at the line in his blue-and-white uniform, bounced the ball a couple of times, took a deep breath, then let fly.

The ball hit the back rim and bounced off.

He went through the same routine, shot the ball, and it hit the rim softly, seemed for an instant like it was going in, and instead rolled off the rim.

Nyblom called time out.

"WARM UP THE BUS. . . . WARM UP THE BUS," a group of East Providence kids sitting in the stands chanted.

The time out over, Delonce went back to the foul line and took a couple of deep breaths, trying to calm his racing heart. He stared at the rim as people yelled and screamed. He shot the ball.

It seemed to hit all sides of the rim as it popped around, only to spin out.

Hope went through the customary postgame handshakes, moving through the line silently and devoid of expression, like zombies, then returned to the locker room with the individual little stalls with the white shower curtains and no place to sit. No one said anything, the room funereal. Delonce bent over a shower stall, his head in his hands, distraught.

Manny came over and tried to comfort him. The coaches came over and tapped him on the shoulder. Still, he didn't move.

"There's not a whole lot I can say right now, gentlemen," Nyblom said softly. "It shouldn't have come down to the free throws."

The room was still silent.

"The two guys sitting out tonight for doing something stupid last year cost us," he continued. "We need everyone to win, gentlemen."

The silence hung in the room.

It had been a crushing defeat, one that left them 6–8 in the league, with just three games left, the playoffs now very much in doubt.

But if Nyblom had been low key in a crushed and demoralized locker room, his tone was different three days later. The day after the East Providence loss there had been another nonleague game out of state, this time at East Boston High School, a team Hope had been playing similar games with for years now. It was meant to be great for morale as everyone played and in the big picture the final score didn't count in the Rhode Island Interscholastic League standings. But Hope hadn't played well, and afterward in the locker room Aaron Lynch had said something derogatory to Johnson Weah and Johnson had chased him and put him in a headlock before being pulled off him.

And now on this Monday afternoon in early February, in the middle of another disappointing practice, one in which a couple of kids had walked in late, Nyblom told everyone to sit at center court.

"The way you carry yourself is atrocious," he said, as if making casual conversation. "You act like idiots. The way you treat each other. You act like you don't care, and if you don't care why should we? You're under .500 in the league and you don't seem to care. How many points did I get? How much playing time did I get? That's what you seem to care about. You're an embarrassment to yourselves, and the way you were brought up. You think you can act a certain way and everyone is just going to forget about it."

He pointed to Johnson.

"You pick on him. You bust his balls. If everyone played like him, had his desire, we wouldn't be in the situation we're in now. But you don't think about that.

"We will not make the playoffs if you continue to do what you're doing. But it's not just basketball. The football team should have been more successful. The soccer team. I don't get it. It might be too late for the seniors. But this can't go on, gentlemen. We haven't had a captain in five years, because it's very difficult to tell your peers what to do, to be a real leader."

He pointed to Delonce.

"Did anyone call him over the weekend to see how he's doing? Because here's a guy who busts his ass every day. Any one of his so-called teammates call him? This is what I'm talking about, gentlemen. Basketball is an extension of school, community, life. And you can't go through life sitting on your ass."

He pointed to the four seniors, Manny, Wayne, Delonce, Johnson.

"Money is being handed out, and because you're minorities you have a chance to get some. There are schools that will take a chance on you. But you have to do your part too. Because you don't work hard enough, and you don't respect each other enough. And I know you don't want to hear this. But guess what? I couldn't care less. My job is to prepare you for real life."

He paused.

"And hopefully we can win a few basketball games."

But it wasn't much better later, about a half hour into practice, that Nyblom told Marquis Young to leave the gym. By chance it came on one of the days when his older brother, Malieke, was there, sitting in the first row of the blue bleachers.

"Why?" Marquis Young said. "I didn't do nothin'."

"Leave the gym," Nyblom said, louder.

"I didn't do anything," Young said.

"LEAVE THE GYM," Nyblom said forcefully.

"Why?" Young yelled back. "I didn't do nothin'."

"If you don't leave the gym everyone is going to run until you do."

Marquis Young stood there.

"LINE UP," Nyblom said loudly.

The players went to the far baseline.

"I didn't do nothing," Marquis Young wailed.

"Yes, you did," Nyblom said.

"I DIDN'T," Marquis Young yelled as he started to walk to the door.

Wayne started to defend Marquis.

"Shut your mouth," Nyblom said to him.

It had been an ugly little scene, the first time a player had openly defied Nyblom all season, and because it was Marquis Young it was emotionally loaded, Marquis being Laurence Young's nephew in addition to being Malieke's half brother. Marquis also was the unofficial leader of the group that included Ben Vezele, Eli Lewis, Aaron Lewis, and Quenton Marrow, all of whom lived in the same neighborhood in South Providence. He didn't get a lot of playing time, and it had become obvious that this bothered him, as if he weren't living up to his family's storied basketball lineage. But he was a good student on a team where too few of his teammates were, said his ambition was to one day be a lawyer just as one of his grandfathers had been, and always was a presence even if the relationship between him and Nyblom had become complicated. That was no insignificant issue because Nyblom has a longtime relationship with Marquis's family, which is why he had attended the funeral of Laurence Young back in December of 2011.

CHAPTER THIRTEEN

The T-shirts were white and baggy and had "A.F.P." in big blue letters on them.

"What's that stand for?" one of the kids asked Keith Moors in the coach's office.

"It's the new team slogan," Moors said.

"What do the letters mean?" the kid asked.

"Argue. Fight. Pout," Moors said. "Because that's what we do."

It was a late Tuesday afternoon in February, another gray winter day, the sky the color of lead. Hope was about to entertain Classical in another key game in their quest to make the playoffs. Their record was now 6-8. The coaches' thinking was that they were going to have to win at least two more games. Wasn't this what had happened last year, a dysfunctional team that finally had found itself in the last weeks of the season, made the playoffs, and gone all the way to the state finals, where they had lost to Central? And if Wayne Clements hadn't been suspended from the team for having stolen a ball at East Providence, wouldn't they have been state champions?

The most frustrating thing of all was the sense that each season began as a clean slate, devoid of memory, devoid of history, as though all the lessons of the past had to be learned over and over again.

So for Nyblom and his assistant coaches it had become all about getting into the state tournament, because that, too, started with a clean slate, another chance for redemption.

But they weren't in yet.

"I believe 2-2 gets us in," Nyblom said as he put soda and Gatorade into the old white refrigerator, even if "6-8, NO PLAYOFFS" was on the blackboard in the hallway, where the players couldn't miss seeing it. Hope was in the middle of six teams in danger of not making the playoffs, right there with Woonsocket, Smithfield, South Kingstown, St. Ray's, and Central.

Next door in the locker room the players were getting into their white uniforms with blue-and-gold trim. Once again, each kid seemed to be wearing different-colored socks, as if their socks and sneakers had become their personal statement. Wayne had bright orange sneakers and yellow socks, Ben bright yellow socks. Johnson no socks. Delonce was lying down in one corner of the room with a headset on.

"You got to be Rondo tonight, Wayne," Manny said, a reference to the Celtics' talented point Rajon Rondo.

"Rondo?" Wayne shot back. "Rondo? Why do I want to be Rondo?"

"This really is the Me Generation," Rob Whalen said, rolling his eyes.

"This isn't Team Building," Nyblom said as he walked into the room. "This is Ugly Sock Day."

He stood facing the team, the players sitting on a bench in front of him.

"We can look at this all you want. We can draw up plays all you want. But we're going to play a big game, and the most important thing? Are we going to play smart? Are we going to play as a team, whether you play the entire game or just one minute? I can't make you do it. You have to do it. And it's real simple. If you want this game more than Classical does, you will win. So who is going to step up and be a leader?"

He turned to the three other coaches.

"Four games left," said Rob Whalen. "Four games. The window is closing fast."

"You've played against all these guys forever," said Jim Black. "You know you can beat them."

"Your season is on the line," Moors said.

But two minutes later, after the team had left the locker room and went up the stairs and into the gym, Moors just shook his head.

"We get blown out tonight by twenty," he said disgustedly. "There's no sense of urgency. They don't want it enough."

Rob Whalen shook his head.

"They don't care about consequences," he said. "There's no fear."

By halftime they were down fourteen and back in the Health Room near the gym, with Nyblom imploring them to play with more passion, more heart, for they had seemed lost and almost bewildered by Classical's zone. Most surprisingly, Manny and Delonce had not started the game, which spoke to some sort of punishment, though no one seemed to know what it meant.

"How many have they got?" Nyblom asked the coaches. "Forty-four? They've got forty-four points at the half, gentlemen? What, we're going to give them a hundred points? It was sixty the last time we played."

He wore his frustration on his face, as the players sat there in front of him.

"Think," he said. "Think basketball, gentlemen. This is the whole season right here."

It worked.

Hope was a different team in the second half, more intense, more focused. They were showing that they usually played together when challenged and when Nyblom got in their faces. They clawed back into the game, tying it at seventy with a Ben three-pointer, and then Manny hit a three-pointer in the dying seconds to get to within one point. But it wasn't enough, as they lost 79-75 in what had been a very good high school game.

"Another game where we didn't start the way we should have," Nyblom said in the Health Room afterward. "Another game where we didn't listen."

He paused, and when he spoke again his words seemed as blunt and direct as running into a blindside screen.

"This game was lost on the opening tip when a coach can't put the team out on the floor that should be on the floor," he said, a reference to Manny and Delonce, who hadn't started for some reason that was yet to be understood.

"And I don't want your shithead friends upstairs running their mouths," he said, looking coldly at Manny and Delonce. "Tell them to shut up, or you will never play."

He stopped, clearly frustrated. Yes, his team was better than it had been earlier in the season. But now they were 6-9 in the league, the playoffs beginning to look as far away as Oz, and he had just lost a huge game where he had not started Manny Kargbo or Delonce Wright, his best player and one of his most dependable players. Here they were with just three games left to play in the league schedule, and to him it still too often seemed, after all the practices and all the pregame talks and all the counseling sessions and all the hopes and dreams, that this could have been a truly magical season, that it was always two steps forward and two steps back. This was a team too often spinning in its own space.

But here in this big drafty room with the anti-drug slogans on the wall and the windows that looked out into the dark night, the team came together in a circle, their arms around each other's shoulders as they hollered out, "On, two, three, HOPE, four, five, six, BLUE WAVE."

It was the next afternoon when some of the answers of the night before were answered.

It started when I walked into the gym just minutes before practice was due to begin.

"Come with me," Nyblom said, his face grim. "This could be the end of the season right here."

"What's going on?" I asked.

"Manny's done," he said. "And his mother's on the way here."

Since the season had begun I had heard references to Manny getting high before school, one of the supposed reasons he had been in such a funk in the beginning of the year. But he had seemed appreciably better since around Christmas, the word being that his father had come up from Delaware and had put some fear into him. Now Nyblom was telling me that he was doing it again and if it took taking basketball away from him to make him stop, than he was going to take basketball away from him, the season be damned.

A few minutes later Manny's mother walked into the gym, a pregnant woman in a gray coat and a smooth, unlined face. A few minutes later they all walked down the stairs and into the Health Room, Manny and his mother, Nyblom and Pedro Correia. Manny looked sad and forlorn, his mother apprehensive.

"This is not the first time, Manny," Nyblom said, his voice low. "You know why we're all here, and this has gotten old.

We're trying to help you. If I put you out there on the court knowing you are high I am not doing my job."

The room was quiet. Manny's mother just looked at Nyblom intently. Nyblom continued.

"My son idolizes you, Manny. What kind of parent am I if I continue to put you out there knowing what you're doing? Other people have tried to talk to you. But you don't listen. You don't see it as a problem. People follow you. Little kids look up to you. And you're going to take all those kids down with you? There has to be consequences. So the only thing I know to do is take basketball away from you. Because that's the only thing that's going to hurt."

Silence hung in the room.

Manny was wearing jeans, sneakers, and a dark blue windbreaker. His mother hadn't taken off her coat.

"You don't think a high school kid getting high is a serious problem?" Nyblom continued. "That's the problem right there. You don't think it's a problem."

He looked at Manny's mother.

"How do you think she feels?"

Manny mumbled something that was inaudible. He fidgeted in his seat.

"Last year you used to come to school early, go in the weight room, get some shots up," Nyblom said. "No more."

The silence continued to hang in the room, Manny with his head down, his mother looking at Nyblom.

"I love you like a son, Manny," Nyblom said, the emotion in his voice. "You want to be the captain, but every day Quenton takes everything downstairs by himself after practice. Every day he acts like a captain. You?"

He shrugged.

"Everyone has bad days. But Pedro and I don't go out and get stoned when we have them."

Pedro Correia looked at Manny, anguish on his face.

"I had a brother, Manny. He had great potential," he said, with tears in his eyes. "He's dead. I'm not lying to you, Manny. On my mother's soul I'm not lying to you. And it breaks my heart to see what you're doing to yourself."

Correia paused.

"You think about it, Manny."

"We get so emotional because there are people who love you," Nyblom said. "Your family. Your coaches. Your team. You have people who love you, but you don't love them back."

He paused again.

"So you get twenty points in a game. What does that mean? I don't know. You tell me what it means. Because if it was so important you wouldn't be screwing it up. You say basketball's important. But it seems getting high is more important than basketball."

Again, the room fell silent.

"Look what you're doing to your mother," Nyblom said. "You're disrespecting your mother."

"I've never disrespected my mother," Manny said with emotion, the first time he had spoken.

"You are right now," Correia said. "Because you're embarrassing her right now."

Manny looked at his mother, pained.

"Anything you ask, I do. I clean the house. I do everything. Every little thing I do."

"Manny," Nyblom said. "You have to go home with your mother and discuss this. If you can't do that, I can't help you. And if you can't come to school without getting high, and you can't play basketball without getting high, you have a real problem."

He then addressed Manny's mother.

"I'd rather lose if it's going to stop him from smoking pot."

You could hear the sounds of sirens in the distance.

CHAPTER FOURTEEN

Senior Night.

It has long been a staple of both college and high school basketball, the symbolic end of careers. Hope was no exception.

So Nyblom stood at half court before the game on a night when there was a good crowd in the small gym and introduced the five seniors. Aaron Lynch, who had moved to Providence with his father shortly before school had started in the fall, got a big hug from his father, a large black man in a dark coat. Aaron was six-foot-two and a good medium-range jump shooter, the kind of kid who would have benefited greatly from another year of high school eligibility. On this team he was behind Manny, Johnson, and Ben, so he didn't get a lot of playing time. But he was well liked, one of the guys, someone who had had no difficulty fitting in.

Delonce Wright came out to the center of the court with his mother and his two little sisters. Johnson Weah came out with his mother. Wayne Clements came out with his father, mother, and little brother. The parents were all given flowers.

Then came Manny, by himself.

He was immediately surrounded by his four teammates, in an obvious show of support.

They posed for pictures taken by Keith Moors and Rob Whalen. They did a "Blue Wave" cheer at center court. The National Anthem was played over the P.A. system.

It had been a nice ceremony, one that spoke to tradition and being a part of something greater than yourself. It spoke to being a Hope basketball player and being part of a large fraternity that went back through the school's long history, all the things Nyblom was always trying to enforce in an era when too few seemed to know or care anything about history.

The five seniors started the game.

Then Hope went out and beat East Providence to run their record to 7-9, still alive for a playoff spot.

"Thank your parents for being here," Nyblom told them afterward in the Health Room.

It had been a great night, one in which the team seemed both focused and together. No arguing. No pouting. A night when it seemed that maybe the team was finally starting to gel.

"If you didn't play a whole lot it's nothing you did wrong," Nyblom continued. "We can't regress, gentlemen, by showing up late. We have to be a team, whether you play or not."

He stopped, looked around.

"Make sure we've got the 'Argue, Fight, Pout' shirts," he added.

Central High School, on the west end of downtown across I-95, sat next to Classical, and was another red-brick school that spoke of another time. Forty years ago it had been the state's high school basketball power, the embodiment of the city game. Marvin Barnes, the former All American at Providence College and the second pick in the 1974 NBA Draft, had gone there, and throughout the '70s Central had dominated the Interscholastic League, full of kids who had streaked across the sports pages of the *Providence Journal*, only to disappear almost as quickly. One had been Levan Anderson, uncle of Quenton Marrow.

The great teams had come in the mid-'70s, after Marvin Barnes had left to self-destruct in the old American Basketball Association, one of basketball's all-time squandered-potential stories. There had been four key players, two lightning-quick little guards, two six-foot-four forwards, four talented kids whom everyone in Rhode Island basketball knew. The basketball world was opening up for inner-city players, and the hope at the time was that maybe they would transcend the Rhode Island Interscholastic League and go off somewhere to have the careers their talent promised. In all the important ways they never did, even though all four had great success at the Community College of Rhode Island, a two-year junior college.

Ultimately, though, none of the four was ever really able to transcend the neighborhood, to truly cash in on the promise. Years later I had done a newspaper story on them, the common theme being one of loss and opportunities that had come and gone, leaving only dusty trophies, the faded echoes of old cheers, and the sense that something important had gotten by them and was never coming back.

But those days were past and now Central was just another inner-city Providence high school basketball team, good some years, not so good the others, the glory days distant memories. Last year they had won the state title at the Ryan Center at the University of Rhode Island, beating Hope in overtime.

Central played its games across a side street from the school in a new, spacious building called the PCTA, on a court bordered by the sidelines of two other courts and a track that circled all the courts. It housed what once were called the commercial courses in high schools: trade classes, business classes, a curriculum geared to prepare kids for jobs. The kind of classes that Hope no longer provided, with everything being geared to prepare kids for college, the new American educational goal. No matter that Nyblom, among others, believed that Hope had flourished when there had been more varied opportunities, instead of trying to funnel everyone into college. Spectators sat upstairs, too far from the court, and on this night there weren't many of them; it felt as if the game were being played in a warehouse.

The irony was that most of the Hope players lived close to Central, Delonce Wright only a few hundred yards away, so if there were neighborhood schools they would be playing for Central. None of them seemed to know of Central's basketball heritage. And if they did, they certainly didn't care.

"Even our kids don't really know anything about it," said Peter Rios, the Central athletic director and football coach. "It's sad. We're trying to bring it back."

The first time I met Rios he had told me a story I've never forgotten. The Central football team was going down Route 195 in neighboring Massachusetts, on their way to play a team in eastern Rhode Island, when they had to cross the Braga Bridge, roughly a half hour east of Providence.

"Look, we're in Cuba!" one kid had yelled out.

"That's not Cuba, you idiot," another one had answered. "That's Puerto Rico."

To me, it was just one more example that too many of these kids lived in their own little bubbles, devoid of history, devoid of geography, clueless about things you would assume high school kids would know, even ones relatively new to this country.

"This is a big, big game," Moors said now in the locker room, minutes before the game. "And you guys don't seem to get it. Everyone's disrespecting you guys. Again in the paper. It's in the sports page every week, you being disrespected. You're either getting trashed, or you're not in it at all. Every day I hear it. Why do you coach those guys? What do you waste your time for? I heard it today. So when are you going to prove everyone wrong?"

He paused, then started in again, his voice louder.

"This is it. We're not going to lose no more. Every game from here on out we're going to win. Every one. We're losing no more games. There were a lot of tears last year in the Ryan Center when we lost. That shit's not going to happen anymore."

Moors began to pass out white T-shirts he had bought with his own money. On the front was a picture of last year's Classical team holding the state championship trophy in the Ryan Center at the University of Rhode Island shortly after they had beaten Hope to win the state championship. They were all jubilant.

"That should have been your trophy," he said. "How do you like looking at it?"

At halftime Hope was up by nine in a ragged game that had all the atmosphere of a closed scrimmage. But Wayne Clements obviously was in some sort of funk, discontent seemed like a virus everyone had caught, and Nyblom was yelling in a time out.

"Stop bitching at each other. End of story."

He turned to Wayne.

"Stop sulking," he said. "If you don't get your head out of your butt we're going to get beat."

A few minutes into the second half he took Wayne out and Wayne walked across the court and went to the end of the bench without even a glance at the coaches. He put his warmup jacket over his head, as if in exile. Nyblom called another time out, the team huddled around him, while Wayne stayed at the far end of the bench with his jacket over his head.

This had been coming for a while, of course. From the first day of practice back in early December he had been, in many ways, the metaphor for the entire season. Hope so desperately needed Wayne Clements to be in the lineup, a senior point guard and the only consistent three-point shooter on the roster. Moors was always calling him the "forty-year-old point guard," which at one level poked fun at the way he often seemed to play with a minimum of effort, and at another acknowledged there was something very old-school about his game, from his stationary shooting, to the way he changed speeds, to the smart way he played, as if he were a reincarnation of a bygone basketball era, one more team-oriented and rooted in fundamentals.

But there had been his knee injury, and Nyblom believed that he wasn't serious enough about his rehabilitation. And from the beginning there was the sense that he too often was emotionally disengaged, complicated by the fact that the coaches believed that if Clements hadn't been caught stealing the ball at East Providence and been suspended from the team for the state tournament last year, Hope would have won the state championship. There was no question of how important Wayne Clements was to them. Hope had started to change their season around as soon as he had started playing, and when he was lost in a personal funk, Hope struggled. Now he sat by himself at the end of the bench with his warmup jacket over his head, a visible symbol of his disengagement.

What was up with Wayne?

Sometimes it seemed impossible to know.

He had grown up with the game, as his father, James "Buster" Clements, had been a high school star at Central in the '70s. Now his father helped run a recreation facility in South Providence referred to as Sackett Street. Wayne had grown up with both Malieke and Marquis Young, and Ben Vezele and Quenton Marrow, too. He had played AAU for Team Providence as a kid. And there's no question he had big basketball dreams, one of those young kids who fantasized about one day playing in the NBA. He had wanted to go to St. Andrew's, the Rhode Island private school with a great basketball tradition, but his grades hadn't been good enough—he had bunked school a lot as an eighth-grader at Gilbert Stuart, and on the days he did come the principal was always chasing him and his friends as they tried to run away from school.

He had never really wanted to go to Hope in the first place, had heard that there were gangs there. But he had liked freshman year, even if he had been so nervous he had thrown up at tryouts. The next year, midway through the season, Nyblom had wanted to put him on the varsity team, but he decided to stay on the jayvee team instead, for he felt comfortable there.

Now he admitted that his knee injury in the summer had depressed him, that he knew he wasn't going to be ready for the season. He had hurt it at the West End Recreation Center, across the street from Gilbert Stuart Middle School, and right away he knew it was serious. He soon realized that it was going to impact his senior year, one that he'd had such high hopes for. He had visualized himself being the state's Gatorade Player of the Year. He had visualized winning the state championship, being All State, having a great season. All the things that now seemed as far away as the moon as he sat on the end of the bench with a towel over his head.

Now he was frustrated, because his knee wasn't what it once had been. He knew he was slower, didn't jump as well. And he was frustrated because he thought it was a selfish team, and he didn't like being on a selfish team. Not that he disliked his teammates. Far from it. He was friendly with all of them, even though he didn't really hang out with any of them. But his senior year was coming undone, with this sense that both fate and the basketball gods had played some cruel trick on him.

So now he sat at the end of bench with his warmup jacket over his head, a basketball Napoleon on some personal Elba.

Nyblom pointed to Johnson, who had just received a technical foul for saying something to one of the referees.

"I told you to shut your mouth. But you don't listen. Now you can't play Friday because of the technical you got."

"I didn't say anything," Johnson said.

"Shut your mouth," Nyblom said.

He pointed to Wayne, still in self-imposed exile down the bench.

"Now he's sulking, and I have no idea how to help that kid," he said, the frustration in his voice.

Then Nyblom turned to Devante Youn, who was in the game to replace Johnson.

"You've taken too many days off," he said. "That's why you're not in shape."

Youn started to say something.

"What?" Nyblom said. "I can't coach you, either?"

A few minutes later, Wayne still at the end of the bench, Marquis Young went down and sat next to him. He put his arm around Wayne's shoulder and his face right next to his ear, and as the game went on in front of them, he continued to talk to Wayne, continued to comfort him. In many ways they had grown up together, in the same neighborhood in South Providence, both attending Gilbert Stuart Middle School, named for the Rhode Island–born artist who had painted George Washington's portrait. And now, Marquis Young, who just several days earlier had suffered his own meltdown at practice, was helping Wayne with his.

In a sense Marquis had seemed better since his recent outburst in practice, as if he had needed to blow off some steam over his frustration with not playing a lot. For he too had his big basketball dreams, just like all the kids. Not surprising. In so many ways it was their identity, this strange dance of young black males and basketball, as if the game belonged to them. Wasn't that the common perception, one fueled by both numbers and stereotypes, the widespread belief that basketball was a black game? Wasn't that the obvious message every time the NBA was on television? Wasn't that the message every time a major college game was on television? Wasn't that your supposed birthright if you were a young inner-city black male?

But what if you simply were not talented enough?

"I knew I wasn't going to play a lot," Marquis Young had said recently. "So I try and treat basketball like a hobby."

He had paused a beat.

"I thought I was better than I was," he had said. "I thought I had to live up to something. Because of my brother. Because of my uncle. I started playing as a young kid with Ben and Wayne and Quenton. I wanted to go to Hope because of my brother."

He also played football at Hope, and he had more success in that sport, but on this night against Central, when he comforted a troubled Wayne, he displayed his best quality as a Hope basketball player.

Hope won the game by nineteen to improve their league record to 8-9, with one league game left to play, and Nyblom was telling them to be smart and go straight home because very few of his players and the jayvee players were going back on the bus to Hope.

"Go home tonight and be on time tomorrow," he said. "It's the last day of school before vacation. And we have to start becoming a team, gentlemen. I don't want to yell at Wayne. I don't want to yell at anyone. But we've got to start doing the right thing. Because we're running out of time."

The surprising thing, at least to me, was that Manny had played in the last two games, for it had seemed that afternoon in the Health Room with his mother that he was done. I didn't say anything to Nyblom about it, though, considered it not my business. Months later, when the season was over, I asked him about it.

"Pedro asked me to take him back," Nyblom said. "That Manny needed it."

He paused then, as if searching for the right words.

"I would never say no to Pedro," he said.

Pedro Correia might be as much Hope as anyone, and it's more than the fact that he has worked there for thirty-five years now. He had grown up on Camp Street, back when everyone seemed to know everyone and there always seemed to be something to do.

"To me it was beautiful," he said. "Then again, I didn't have to worry about going out and getting shot."

His father worked for a contractor who did a lot of work at nearby Brown University. His family was stable, and from the fourth through the seventh grade he went to school at Holy Name, the big stone Catholic church on Camp Street. He then went to Nathan Bishop, the neighborhood middle school for the East Side, then to Hope. He arrived in the fall of '68, and the following spring there were the riots at Hope that, in retrospect, changed the school forever, though no one could have predicted it at the time.

"Kids wanted curriculum change, and they wanted more relevant courses," he said. "I was more aware of everything changing. The death of Martin Luther King. It was all sad. But I didn't see Camp Street change back then. It was still a community, a neighborhood. I never had any fear."

He played basketball at Hope, at a time when Central was the best high school team in the state. It was the first time in Rhode Island that an inner-city Providence school had put its indelible stamp on the Rhode Island Interscholastic League.

Central was coached by a black man named Jimmy Adams, who had gone from Hope to the University of Rhode Island, where he became a football star. The first real star who made the leap from the Providence 'hood to the basketball big-time was a skinny kid named Marvin Barnes, who followed Adams to Providence College, where he had become an assistant coach to Dave Gavitt. Eventually, Gavitt would go on to form the Big East Conference, while Barnes became one of the all-time basketball cult figures. High school basketball was changing, just as Providence was starting to change.

Correia went to Rhode Island College because his family set the tone.

"Both my father and mother worked, and it was expected that I go to college," he said.

In 1978 he began working at Hope, first with the jayvee team, and helping out then-coach Jerry Morgan. He soon came to realize that everything was different, noting the demise of many of the rec leagues that had been part of the glue of the neighborhoods, places run by strong men who were community leaders. For all the societal change, many people were left behind too, whether by drug abuse that swept through many of Providence's neighborhoods, by a tough economy, or just by change that came too quickly. Regardless of the reasons, it was now decades later and Pedro Correia said he wouldn't want to be a kid these days, that there were too many kids constantly maneuvering through an obstacle course he never had to deal with.

"It's much more difficult for kids now, and I'm not even talking about the ones who have no clue. I'm glad I didn't have to take two buses to school and have to go through Kennedy Plaza every day, because you just don't know down there. I saw things get worse in the early '90s. We played some football games where no spectators were allowed. Now we have kids who have

'safety transfers' because if they stay in their schools they fear for
their well-being. I had a kid a while back who was afraid to go
play at Central. I have kids say they can't even have a girlfriend
in a different part of the city because it's too dangerous."

And maybe what hurt him the most was that too many kids
placed no value in education, for he knew that education changed
his life.

"The last fifteen years it's harder to keep kids eligible. They
just don't see it as a priority. But they know every rapper. Where
they live. What they eat. Everything about them. But then they
walk across that stage to get that diploma on graduation night,
and now what?"

Another practice in February looking for a spark. It was nearing
the end of the season and there had been too many practices, both
for Nyblom and the players.

Only four players showed up in the beginning, with a few
guys in Credit Recovery—and a couple others meeting with
teachers. Some alumni were there too.

"Urgency?" said Keith Moors. "I don't see it."

Instead, it all seemed like a season that was playing itself out,
ending not in any big dramatic flourish, but in a succession of
small endings.

"Can we ever do anything right?" an exasperated Nyblom
asked about an hour later.

"We are doing it right," said Delonce Wright.

"No, you're not."

So Nyblom made them run laps around the gym, Wayne
last, running like he was sixty-five years old, in white shorts and
a red Miami Heat T-shirt.

"We're running out of time, gentlemen!" Nyblom yelled out.

Moors and Rob Whalen sat in the first row of the bleachers.

They had seen this all before, of course, another a team that seemed to squander its talent almost daily.

"This is typical Hope," Whelan said, rolling his eyes. "They'll start to figure it out when they leave."

This was Whelan's sixth season as a volunteer assistant, and from the beginning he had loved it. Loved being around a team every day. Loved Nyblom and Moors. He had grown up in Elmhurst, close to Providence College and La Salle, and played in the very competitive Providence CYO league for the famed Armand Batastini, who had coached St. Pius seemingly since the beginning of time. Then he had played at Classical for the very successful Don Pastine, and later at Roger Williams, a Division III school in Rhode Island, for my childhood friend and high school teammate Mike Raffa. In many ways it was a basketball experience out of old Rhode Island, one that had included learning the game the right way, but when Whelan first started volunteering he quickly learned that the landscape had changed.

"I probably hadn't been to a high school game in twenty years when I started at Hope," he said. "And when I had played at Classical in high school Hope was a very tough place to play, an intimidating place. But the biggest surprise was that so many kids really had no idea how to play the right way. When they came out for the team it was like they had never really been coached before. And it was like you had to all but scream to get their attention. I was surprised at how Hope had changed in that regard. In the beginning I guess I thought it would be easier to get through to them. But too few of them take advantage of what's available to them."

Whelan quickly learned to like the kids, though, realized they were all good kids one-on-one, but so many were dragged down by the collective mentality, the forces waiting right outside the gym's doors. The peer pressure. The family issues. A brutal culture that seemed to be their biggest opponent.

Hope players wear assorted kicks to play — nothing uniform here.

(Courtesy of Bob Breidenbach)

Senior Aaron Lynch, wearing a T-shirt with the Blue Wave's motto, has a ready smile for teammate Wayne Clements.

(Courtesy of Bob Breidenbach)

Volunteer assistant coach Rob Whalen has a locker room chat with sophomore Eli Lewis. *(Courtesy of Bob Breidenbach)*

Keith Moors, one of Hope's three volunteer assistant coaches, takes the team's temperature before a game. *(Courtesy of Bob Breidenbach)*

The Blue Wave lines up for the national anthem before a playoff game at Providence College. *(Courtesy of Bob Breidenbach)*

Senior point guard Wayne Clements taking the ball up the court.

(Courtesy of Bob Breidenbach)

Never shy about making a point, Hope Coach Dave Nyblom has a word
with a referee. *(Courtesy of Bob Breidenbach)*

Senior star Manny
Kargbo on defense.

*(Courtesy of Bob
Breidenbach)*

Johnson Weah, surrounded by his teammates, makes a pregame point. Delonce Wright is to left of Weah. On the right are Eli Lewis, Angel Rivera, and Wayne Clements. *(Courtesy of Bob Breidenbach)*

Sophomore guard Eli Lewis takes the ball up the court.

(Courtesy of Bob Breidenbach)

Sophomore Angel Rivera practices his free throw shooting in Hope High School's aging gym. *(Courtesy of Bob Breidenbach)*

Senior Delonce Wright lines up a shot during practice at Hope High School.

(Courtesy of Bob Breidenbach)

The Blue Wave in high, team-raising spirits before a game at the University of Rhode Island's Ryan Center. *(Courtesy of Bob Breidenbach)*

Coach Nyblom outlines a play during a timeout in a playoff game.

(Courtesy of Bob Breidenbach)

Coach Nyblom consoles sophomore Angel Rivera following a loss.

(Courtesy of Bob Breidenbach)

He also quickly learned that, yes, he was volunteering at a Providence high school, but it certainly wasn't the Classical of his own high school experience.

Maybe it was the day a kid named Mookie threw a trash can on the floor, or the time a kid practiced in socks and no sneakers, and that was just the way it was. He was in a brave new basketball world, a new landscape nothing had prepared him for.

Whelan soon came to love it, though, to look forward to coming to practice every late afternoon, every day a new adventure. He was needed here in ways he wouldn't be in a suburban coaching situation, or at one of the parochial schools. In so many ways, coaching at Hope was like coaching nowhere else. For there was something very compelling about it, too, the reason he always looked forward to coming to practice. Even on those dysfunctional afternoons when it seemed as if Hope's biggest opponent was themselves.

'Last year was the same thing," Moors said. "All the same shit. Then we went down to play at North Kingstown and played a great game out of nowhere, and that was the key. It was like we found ourselves as a team that night. After that we went on a crazy run. Wild stuff happened, and we just kept winning games. And if Wayne didn't get himself suspended we would have been state champions. And you know what? We're better now. Have got more talent."

He hesitated, looked out at the court, at the players going through drills.

"But it's not about talent. It's about all the other things. It's about 'Argue, Fight, Pout.' We're 8-9 in the league right now, and we haven't won a state title since 1995. But it's always something."

Moors had seen that "something" from the moment he had volunteered to help Nyblom six years ago. In hindsight, it was the thing that had surprised him the most. For he had thought coaching was going to be about basketball. But now he had come to believe that it wasn't about all the things that happened on the court, as much as all the things that happened off it.

"You never really know what happens once they leave the school," he said, "because they don't like to talk about it. But they bring it into the gym with them, so you know it's something."

Moors knew the kids in ways the other coaches didn't. His mother had battled drug problems when he was growing up, his father was not in his life, and he'd known at a subliminal level that he had to figure it out for himself. In many ways, basketball had saved him. It had provided him with a good high school experience, which had led him to a junior college outside of Boston. That, in turn, had taken him to Eastern Connecticut State University, where he'd been exposed to a different world than the one his parents had lived in, and it had changed him.

So now the coaches and player were down to the last game of the regular season, a home game against Cranston East that they had to win if they were going to get to .500 and qualify for the playoffs. Once again they were gathered in the Health Room, a huge game a half hour away. And once again, Nyblom didn't like their body language.

"I really don't like our attitude," he said. "It's very casual in here. This could be our last game, gentlemen. Anyone want to say anything?"

He looked at Wayne.

Wayne shook his head.

He looked at Manny.

"No," Manny said.

He looked at Aaron Lynch.

Lynch shook his head.

He looked at Johnson.

Johnson didn't respond, just stared straight ahead.

He looked at Delonce.

"Play hard," Delonce said softly.

The game against Cranston East a few weeks earlier had been rough and nasty, as if always just a few minutes away from a fight. This one began the same way, two teams playing rough and physical, with all the intensity of a playoff game. Then again, for Hope, it practically was. To get to the playoffs they had to win. It was that simple. Do or die.

Near the end of the first half Manny scored on a nifty drive to the basket. Nyblom quickly called time out and picked up the microphone from the scorer's table next to him.

"Manny Kargbo just scored the one thousandth point of his high school career," he said to the crowd.

The ball was given to Manny, the people in the small gym cheered, his teammates surrounded him, and Manny had a big smile on his face.

But the team was in a dogfight with Cranston East.

They were up 24-21 at the half, back in the Health Room, and the talk was of Manny scoring his one thousandth point.

"I just want to get *one* point," quipped Marquis Young.

Tension hung over the second half in another close nail-biter of a game. It was there on the faces of the coaches, as each miss, each mistake, each time Cranston East scored, the pressure ratcheted up another notch. This long season that had started last summer at the PCTA downtown in a summer league, then continued in the fall league, then started again in earnest when practice had begun in early December, had now come down to these last few minutes ticking off the two small scoreboards mounted on the walls of this old gym that had seen so many games since it first opened in 1936.

"Stop, both of you!" Nyblom yelled at Manny and Wayne, who were upset with each other. "You're acting like little kids. This is a playoff game."

Then, after another missed free throw, Nyblom turned to the bench and all but barked, "How many of you guys stay after practice and take some extra free throws after practice?"

He stared at them.

"That would be zero."

Midway through the half Eli Lewis came into the game and quickly gave Hope a spark, as they went up nine with roughly eleven minutes left to play. There was no question that Eli was talented. He was quick, left-handed, able to dunk on a break even though he was under six feet tall. To look at Eli was to see his vast potential, this kid who had showed up in the beginning of the year from Connecticut like an unexpected gift left on the doorstep. Yet he was also the personification of the young, inner-city player. He was unfocused, hypersensitive to any kind of criticism, unable to look at the person addressing him, as if even the least little hint of criticism were an assault.

"I'm not criticizing you, Eli," Nyblom would say, "I'm trying to coach you."

But to Eli it was the same thing.

Later, he would admit that without basketball he'd be hanging out with the wrong crowd, that without basketball he'd be in trouble. The year before, he had been in high school in Bridgeport, Connecticut, but now he was here with his mother and little sister in South Providence, living right down the street from Ben, the first kid he had met in his new city, and also near Marquis Young and Quenton Marrow. He had started at Hope in November after almost going to Central, which was near his house.

Basketball was very important to him, as if the game gave his life meaning.

"I don't know where I'd be without it," he said. "Without it I just feel empty."

He would also admit months later that his attitude had been terrible, that "you can't tell me anything." That he used to talk back to teachers in middle school, and that if he went to school and something negative happened he was mad for the entire day.

Then there was his father, who lived in Connecticut.

"I talk to him once in a while, but he's not around," he said. "But I don't care anymore. He used to lie to me. When he calls now I don't even want to speak to him. Because if he's not going to teach me how to be a man then why should I listen to him?"

He paused.

"I'm trying to bring myself up," he said firmly. "I'm trying to teach myself how to be a man."

Still, on this night Eli Lewis had given Hope a big lift, someone off the bench who could affect a game.

But five minutes later Hope was clinging to a slim three-point lead.

"Do you want to win?" Nyblom yelled during a time out, his face flushed. "Because right now you're playing to lose. This is your season. Right here."

The game seesawed back and forth as the minutes fell off the clock. Up one. Down one. Up one. And all the while there was Nyblom like a jockey trying to get his horse to the finish line, a whip here, a whip there, the season hanging in the balance.

Then they were down one, with just twenty-five seconds left, and in a time out.

"You're acting like you've lost already," Nyblom said, his face flushed. "Pick yourself up."

Cranston East had the ball and as one of their players drove to the basket for what looked like an easy basket Ben Vezele, who would finish with eighteen points and fifteen rebounds, came out of nowhere and blocked the shot at the rim. After a time out, Hope still down one, Ben missed a short shot at the rim, and then in a moment of great second effort he bounced up to get his own rebound and scored to win the game.

Hope was going to the playoffs.

CHAPTER FIFTEEN

"I think we're the best team in Rhode Island," said Keith Moors.

He was sitting with Rob Whalen and Jim Black in the cramped coach's office, where the clock still said 6:32.

"This is how we play every year," he continued. "We start out lousy, go through all our typical nonsense, and by the end of the year no one wants to play us. That's how it is every year. Like we get locked in. But we're a bad matchup for a lot of teams. Manny gets to the rim against anyone. I think Wayne's locked in now. We're deeper than last year."

Whalen nodded his head.

"We're playing our best at the right time. It's just like last year."

In about an hour they would be playing East Providence in the first round of the playoffs, and there was the palpable sense that this was the start of a brand-new season, as if all the old ghosts of the past ten weeks or so had somehow been exorcised. Manny was in great spirits, had been enthusiastic and energetic in practice, as if a heavy weight had been lifted from his shoulders.

Wayne and the coaches seemed to have had found their separate peace, an unspoken deal in which his obvious uninterest in practice and concern for his knee was overlooked as long as he came to play in the games. It was apparent to everyone that his knee wasn't anywhere close to 100 percent, but he wanted to play and Hope obviously needed him to play. Delonce and Johnson always were steady, always playing hard. And Ben? He had quietly come into his own; he was more confident, more self-assured on the court, his eighteen-point, fifteen-rebound performance and his late-game heroics against Cranston West vivid examples.

The players wandered in and out of the coach's room.

"Nyblom, can I get a water? . . . Nyblom, when you tapin' my ankles? . . . Nyblom, when we going upstairs? . . . Nyblom, where you at?"

On and on it went until Nyblom went to take his pregame shower, and Moors locked the door.

"GO AWAY!" he yelled as someone knocked on the door.

"Where's Nyblom at?" yelled a voice back.

"He's in the shower," Moors yelled back. "Give him a break. Go away. Leave him alone."

Moors laughed.

"They're always bitching about Dave. He's too tough. He yells too much. He's too demanding. Then he goes in the shower for five minutes and they can't function. It never changes."

A half hour later everyone was upstairs in the Health Room in their white "Refuse to Lose" T-shirts over their white uniforms, "A.F.P." on the sleeves, the team slogan. Wayne wore a black beanie in. Nyblom had already taped a few ankles on a table in the small hallway outside the locker room. On a message board behind him were all the East Providence players and what they wanted to do in the game, alongside all of East Providence's tendencies. All things he had gone over already.

"Okay, gentlemen," said Nyblom. "Lose tonight and we go home."

He paused a beat.

"And do not say a word to the referees. Not one word."

He paused again, looked out over them.

"They don't have your depth. They don't have your speed. They didn't go deep into the playoffs last year like you did. Intelligence and desire, gentlemen, intelligence and desire. So play smart, and let's have some fun."

"No team in the state can beat you," added Pedro Correia.

He pointed to Johnson Weah.

"We have the best rebounder in the state."

He pointed to Manny.

"We have the best player in the state."

He pointed to Wayne.

"We have the best point guard in the state."

Not that Hope really needed the pep talk. They were up ten at halftime, fifteen with 10:30 to play, and coasted to the finish. And the next afternoon they were back in the same little gym on the second floor trying to prepare for the same La Salle team that had beaten them earlier in the regular season, the game in which Wayne had sat in self-imposed exile at the end of the bench in the last minutes.

"Showtime's here," Moors yelled out as Wayne walked in, wearing dark blue warmups and a dark blue hood.

Practice was low key, highlighted at one point by a spirited three-on-three half-court game. Wayne sat in the bleachers. He said his knee was sore, and when he walked onto the court he shuffled along like he was sixty years old and coming off a bad night.

"Showtime's here," Moors called out again.

Wayne just stared at him and slowly shook his head.

Moors laughed.

Delonce was at the dentist. Johnson had come late. Everything seemed dialed down, a time out from the pressure. This, too, was part of Nyblom's coaching style. He had come to learn that a team couldn't go hard every day late in the season, that there was no reason to leave your game in the gym. So practices were shorter, often more varied. This one had been very loose, unstructured, and for much of the time Nyblom had been downstairs doing the team's laundry.

Now it ended with everyone sitting at the half-court circle.

"The whole La Salle team was here last night," he said, standing over the players. "We're going to get their best shot."

The playoff game against La Salle was at North Providence High School, an old red-brick building less than a mile away from La Salle and the north end of Providence. It was a neutral court. This was the quarterfinals of the Division I tournament. The opponent was the same La Salle team that easily had beaten Hope in mid-January in the La Salle gym, when Hope had self-destructed with Wayne sulking down at one end of the bench. But there was no question things were different now, with Hope playing better, more as a team than they had been back then. Coventry and Mount Pleasant were playing in the first game while Hope waited downstairs.

Nyblom told them that if they played hard and they played smart and pushed the ball and concentrated on defense they would win the game, and as the team left the locker room all the coaches gave Wayne a pat on the back, for when Wayne played well Hope usually played well.

"Okay, gentlemen, lose tonight and we go home," he said. "And don't say one word to the referees. Not one word."

"Hey, Raymond," Moors said to Raymond Perez, a small ninth-grader with a great smile who had now become the team manager, as the two left the locker room to go up the stairs that led to the court. "Pull your pants up; you look like a hood from the city."

Raymond started walking up the stairs as Moors smiled at him.

"Teams don't want to play us," Moors said. "We're a tough matchup for most teams, and I think Wayne's locked in right now."

The gym was good for a Rhode Island high school, with bleachers on both sides. Tonight it was packed. There were La Salle cheerleaders in red-and-white uniforms. There was a public address system. There was a sense of importance that had been missing in so many of the regular-season games. And at the half Hope was up 32-24, even though they had been 0-8 from the free-throw line.

"When you get the ball just look for the ugliest shoes on the floor," Nyblom said, pointing to Wayne's bright orange sneakers. "That's what you're looking for."

There was no longer any pretense: when the ball was in Wayne Clements's hands everything was smoother. When the ball was in his hands Hope was a better basketball team, orange sneakers or not.

"Keep getting in their face," Pedro Correia implored. "You dominate every team in the state defensively."

The second half was extremely intense, two teams playing for their season to continue, the private Catholic school and the inner-city school, complete with all the stereotypes that come with that distinction. They were two teams that had a little dustup during a fall league game, two teams that didn't seem to have much use for each other even in the best of times, never mind a playoff game. They also had played in last year's state tournament, Hope winning. Three of the La Salle players were from Camp Street, to the point of occasionally spending time in the Hope gym. And in the small, interconnected world of Rhode

Island high school, everyone either knew each other or were a few degrees of separation away.

So it was no surprise that the game was chippy, many of the fouls hard. No surprise that the gym was loud and the emotion seemed to hang over the players' heads like fine mist. For there was little difference between the two teams, and the game could go either way.

La Salle played Manny a box and one, making it much more difficult for him to score, while Hope's tenacious man-to-man defense was making it equally difficult for La Salle. Hope was up four with 6:37 to play, but Wayne had to come out with four fouls, the tension building.

"It's all about winning and playing Friday night," Nyblom implored them in a time out.

And win they did, as both Wayne and Eli Lewis made key free throws in the last two minutes and Hope pulled away to win by fourteen.

But the night was just beginning.

To get to the locker rooms you had to go out the gym, across the lobby, and down some stairs. I was heading toward the stairs, about a minute or two behind the players, when I heard yelling coming from below. By the time I got down the stairs it was chaos—assistant coach Jim Black was bleeding from the mouth, and Arondae Washington, father of La Salle's Keon Wilson and Mikey Clark, was still trying to get at Black.

"No one's going to put his hands on my kid," he yelled.

"Arondae, I was trying to break it up!" Black yelled back.

There was too much confusion, too much milling around, and I had gotten there too late to know what had really happened. A couple of Hope kids were behind Black, and some La Salle kids were behind Arondae Washington, the atmosphere charged up, like kindling just waiting for a match, when Nyblom and Moors came down the stairs and got the Hope players back around the corner and into their locker room.

Inside the locker room the emotion almost seemed to bounce off the walls. It was becoming clear that there had been an altercation between Delonce Wright and Jared Thompson, a white guard from La Salle. What had happened was unclear, at least to me. Johnson Weah had also been involved in something, but that, too, was unclear.

Nyblom was trying to calm the players down, to get them back to the game they had just won and away from what had happened on the stairs, whatever that had been.

"We are very lucky to be advancing," Nyblom said. "So give yourself three claps."

The players clapped three times.

"He got called a 'spic,'" he said, pointing to Angel Rivera.

"He got called a 'nigger,'" he said, pointing to Johnson Weah.

"We've been called everything tonight," he said.

He paused.

"And I don't want anyone texting tonight on what happened. No Facebook. No nothing. Whatever you hear don't chirp back. Stay off your phone."

The players started getting their stuff together, putting their clothes over their uniforms.

"Angel, very solid," Nyblom said. "Johnson, very solid. Manny, very solid. So give yourself three more claps."

Nyblom paused.

"We're all going out together," he said.

"What happened?" I asked Wayne Clements quietly over in a corner of the locker room. "I got there late."

"I was there," he said. "I was trying to stop things."

He laughed.

"It didn't work out."

"Where are the 'Argue, Fight, Pout' shirts?" Nyblom yelled out. "Make sure we've got them."

"Argue, Fight, Pout" had become both an indictment and unofficial team slogan, as if all the dysfunction and all the drama since the opening day of practice had turned into a team slogan, as bizarre as that sounded.

ARGUE.

FIGHT.

POUT.

This team's identity.

But the ramifications of the fight were not over.

The next morning, all the players were in the Hope cafeteria, the cavernous room with red pillars in the middle and tables everywhere. It was vacation week. Sunlight poured into the room from the large windows on the south side of the building. The team sat at four tables, Malieke Young with them.

They were supposed to be writing about the fight, as the school was trying to understand what had happened, but mostly they were laughing and telling war stories from the night before.

"Yo, yo, yo," Delonce said, laughing. "Wayne was like, 'They're fighting? I just got these new braids on.'"

Wayne laughed.

"Jared touched my face during the game," Delonce said. "And then he pushed me coming down the stairs. That started it. It was me, Johnson, Aaron, and Marquis on the stairs, and La Salle was talking shit. Then he pushed me. If anything, Johnson got jumped, and he was trying to be the peacemaker. But the whole thing was like twenty seconds tops. Now La Salle is saying that we won the game and started the fight. But why would we have started a fight if we had won the game? But it's in the past. I'm moving on."

He pointed to the piece of paper in front of him.

"I wrote three sentences. That's all I know."

"They were saying on the stairs that they had no respect for us, and I was saying, 'You lost,'" said Aaron Lynch.

"We beat them in the game. We beat them in the fight. And we still get no respect," said Malieke Young, as if he couldn't understand the indignity of it all.

"He pushed me," Delonce said. "It had been building up since the fall league. Jared had pushed me then and I didn't understand it. Because I know a lot of those guys and always had been cool with them. But it's in the past. I'm moving on. We won the game. That's the best part."

The atmosphere was loose. They were advancing, and the fight had become just war stories, just yesterday's news, right?

Not really.

The next morning it was announced by the Rhode Island Interscholastic League that Delonce Wright and Johnson Weah would be suspended for Hope's next playoff game against Coventry, a team they had lost to early in the season, to be held at the Community College of Rhode Island in Warwick. Hope would get to play another playoff game, only this time without two starters, and to Nyblom it didn't seem right. For he believed his players, believed that La Salle had started the altercation on the stairs because they were upset at having lost the game, and that the suspensions were just the latest example of his program getting disrespected by the Interscholastic League. Yet he also knew there was no recourse, and that now they had to play the hand they'd been dealt, fair or not.

To him, it had come as no big surprise.

It was no secret that the relationship between him and Tom Mezzanotte, the head of the Interscholastic League, was strained at best. To Nyblom, the league's favorites were Hendricken and La Salle, the long-standing parochial school powers, the two

schools with the most clout, the most success, the two deeply imbedded into the state's political hierarchy in ways the public
schools were not, especially the inner-city ones. That was simply the way it was, the way it always it had been, and to fight
against it was like trying to fight City Hall.

The first game of the night at CCRI in Warwick was between
Hendricken and Classical, two teams that had beaten Hope in
the regular season, and when Hope went into their small locker
room "NO RESPECT" was printed on the blackboard in big
letters.

"I can't find my jersey," Wayne said.

Eli Lewis threw a jersey at Wayne from across the room.

"East Side Negroes," Nyblom yelled out.

"Where's Quenton?" asked Rob Whalen. "Where's Q?"

"He's in Virginia," said Marquis Young.

"What's he doing in Virginia?"

"Family trip," Young said.

So now there was no Delonce, no Johnson, and no Quenton,
either. Just nine players in their white T-shirts with "Refuse to
Lose" on the front that they wore over their dark blue uniform
tops. Now they were about to play Coventry in the Division I
semifinals.

"We love all you guys," Nyblom said softly, "and none of
this is fair. But we have the talent to win, even without Delonce,
Johnson, and Quenton. And we have the leadership to win. So
push the ball, and keep pushing it. And if anyone uses the 'N'
word don't react. And if anyone says a thing don't react. We
waited all year to start playing, and now we're playing. And tonight we're going to play for Delonce and Johnson, who don't
deserve this, and we're going to play for Quenton, too."

•   •   •

There was a good crowd in the big gym, the sense of anticipation building. Classical had beaten Hendricken 45-44 in the first game, so the winner of the Hope-Coventry game would go on to play Classical on Sunday afternoon at Brown in the Division I finals, and be all but assured of a good seed in the state tournament that was to follow. But the pregame dramatics weren't over yet. In fact, they were just beginning.

As Hope lined up across the court for the National Anthem there were Manny and Aaron Lynch holding up Delonce's blue jersey with his number 2 on the back, and there were Marquis Young and Eli Lewis doing the same thing with Johnson Weah's uniform with number 23 on it. It was a dramatic moment, and a symbolic one, too. Ever since practice had started back in early December Nyblom had preached about becoming a team, a fragile little ecosystem even in the best of times. That had always been the message from Nyblom and the other coaches, all those times when Hope was going one step forward and two steps back. And now here they were doing something completely unexpected and improvisational, something that went to the core of what a team was all about, symbolically saying that their two teammates were with them in spirit, if not physically. And as I looked out at them, those four players holding up those two jerseys of their absent teammates, I saw it as their shining moment of the season, regardless of what was going to happen in the game.

Not everyone saw it this way, of course.

It was quickly obvious that the officials of the Interscholastic League didn't like it. Then again, the league and Nyblom often seemed to be circling each other like wary alley cats. There was too much bad history, too many times when Nyblom—long a powerful voice for the state's male high school coaches—had clashed with the Interscholastic League. But minutes later, when the game began, Hope moved out to a lead, and then kept it to halftime, up seven as they went back to the small locker room.

"The kid in the ugly-ass orange sneakers is going to lead us," he said, looking at Wayne. "Just keep looking for those ugly-ass sneakers and keep getting him the ball."

"Do it for Delonce and Johnson sitting home right now," Moors said.

With twelve minutes left to play they were up eight, but Wayne had four fouls and was on the bench and Hope was playing with two starters in Manny and Ben and sophomores Angel Rivera and Eli Lewis and senior Aaron Lynch. Could they somehow hang on? Could Angel, Eli, and Aaron, three kids from the bench now in the biggest game of their lives, play up to the moment? Could this ragtag group that really hadn't played together all year hang on long enough to get Hope to Sunday afternoon against Classical for the Division I title? Did they have enough?

Within a minute they were only up one, Coventry back in the game, and Nyblom called time out.

"Manny, Manny," he said. "Don't let up."

He looked around the huddle.

"Great defense, Eli," he said.

Nyblom was supportive, encouraging, imploring Manny and Ben to carry them.

The game moved inexorably toward the finish, Hope always up, but unable to pull away. Up five. Up three. Up seven. Until there was just 1:35 left to play and Hope was only up three, and Nyblom was urging his team on, his face flushed. With twenty-six seconds to play Manny made two free throws, the eventual clinchers, as a group in the bleachers chanted out, "Blue Wave, Blue Wave," and the final score was 65–62.

"They keep trying," said Jim Black in the jubilant locker room. "But they can't keep us down."

Over in the corner of the locker room Wayne had combed out his braids, his hair now a large Afro, circa 1975.

"Look at Frederick Douglass over there," said Rob Whalen, with a big smile. "But if I ask him who Frederick Douglass was he'll say, 'Didn't he play in the NBA?'"

CHAPTER SIXTEEN

It was Sunday morning, two days after Hope had beaten Coventry, and in a few hours they were going to play Classical for the Division I title. But now Nyblom was putting a large container of food in the back of his red Chevy Silverado, the one with 250,000 miles on it. He stood in the driveway of his white house off Broad Rock Road, which goes from the center of South Kingstown and weaves its way to Route 138, the state highway that runs from Route 1 to the University of Rhode Island just a couple of miles away. His brother lives next door. His mother lives two doors down. It is a deeply wooded area, and out behind Nyblom's big field of a backyard there are woods, five acres in all.

"My grandfather came from Finland and bought sixty-seven acres," he said as he got into the truck. "He used to have a Christmas tree farm. This was a dirt road then, and across the street was a couple of Narragansett Indian families. It was called Shantytown. Upper Broad Rock Road. It was the '70s."

"We had our own little compound, the Kennedys of Shantytown," Nyblom said with a smile. "Now my mother has a house. My cousin. My brother. And my older brother around the corner."

He met his wife Tammie on the Fourth of July 1985, down in nearby Narragansett near the Atlantic Ocean. When they got married they moved into a house on the family land because it was close to Wakefield, South Kingstown's business center, yet still felt like the country. His teams come each year for an outing, both boys' basketball and girls' soccer.

"They go outside in the dark and it's always like they're scared shit," he said with a smile. "So I tell them I'll have some bullets go by, and have some people screaming, so they can feel comfortable."

He drives out to Route 138, takes a right, and within a couple of minutes is on Route 1 heading north to Providence.

"When I was a kid going to Providence was a big trip," he said with a shrug. "Now I go every day."

Bringing the food just sort of evolved.

"I started passing it out every once in a while and soon realized that sometimes it was the only thing some of them had eaten all day."

Every few minutes his cell phone rang.

"What time is the bus leaving? I'm going to be late. All the usual stuff," he said of the phone calls that have been his life for over two decades.

He was into North Kingstown now, about a half hour from Providence, and talking about how coaching at Hope has enriched not only his life but his family's life too, exposed them to things they never would have seen if their entire lives had been spent in South Kingstown, to kids who had broadened their worlds.

"I grew up with minorities in South Kingstown," he said, "but it was different then. It was a small town and they had people looking out for them. In many ways back then the community helped raise them. But the first year I was at Hope I had a kid who wore the same clothes every single day. I saw kids who didn't get enough to eat. I saw the kind of poverty I had never seen before. And it's worse now. There used to be more of an infrastructure in the neighborhoods than there is now. Now there are a lot of kids with no place to go. There are days when I have to throw them out of the gym or they wouldn't leave."

We were on I-95 now, heading north, going through War-wick and Cranston, fifteen minutes south of Hope, and Nyblom recalled that from the time he first started teaching at Hope he never found race to be an issue. But he was in his second gen-eration of kids now, and things were worse. From the kids who arrived with elementary school reading levels, to the constant turnover, to the fact that there were innumerable languages spo-ken in the building, there was the increasing sense that things were more difficult now, more hard-edged.

When we arrived at Hope he pulled the red truck into the courtyard and began carrying the big trays of food into the build-ing. Hot dogs. Beans. Pork rolls. By the time the kids showed up shortly afterward the food was in the cluttered room full of weight machines and other paraphernalia between the coach's office and the locker room.

Manny was all dressed up, almost as if he had stepped out of a fashion magazine. Black coat. Black shoes. And a black scarf over a white sweater. Delonce was wearing a bow tie and a gray beanie. Aaron Lynch was in a dark suit and a bow tie. Virtually everyone seemed to have their Sunday best on.

The game was to be in the Brown University gym, part of an athletic grouping that included the hockey arena, a big recre-ation center, and a new red-brick state-of-the-art fitness center. The complex is a couple of blocks from the university's center, across Thayer Street, where so many of the Hope kids walked every day on their way to the bus that took them downtown to Kennedy Plaza, roughly two hundred yards from Hope.

The atmosphere was loose and casual. The talk was of the NBA.

Then Devante Youn walked in with a dark coat and a new close-cropped haircut.

"'Bout time you got rid of that nasty-ass 'fro," said Moors.

Youn laughed.

The only player not there was Wayne.

"Do you know where the Brown gym is?" I asked Manny.

"No," he said.

I asked Ben the same question.

"I have no idea," he said.

Most of the players were devouring the food. A couple were upstairs in the gym shooting around. A yellow school bus that would take them the two hundred yards to the Brown gym waited in the small parking lot in the back of the building.

Then in walked Wayne with his hair in tight braids.

"Twenty-year-old cornrows," said Moors.

A few minutes later the yellow school bus pulled out of the parking lot behind the school, took a right on Hope Street. It slowly began going south, then stopped.

"Okay," Moors yelled out. "Get off."

The trip had taken twenty seconds.

"Can we be quiet, gentlemen?" Nyblom asked as they came into the locker room. "First off, congratulations on getting this far. It wasn't easy. We all know that. But then if it were easy it wouldn't be you guys. But when the lights go on you guys show up. And today the lights are on bright."

They were playing Classical, the same Classical that had beaten them twice in the regular season. The same Classical team full of kids they had grown up playing against in youth leagues and AAU games, and throughout their high school careers. In short, there were no mysteries here. They were peaking at the right time, much of the internal drama behind them. This season was mirroring last year's, the one where they had gotten through the minefield of their own malaise to make it all the way to the state finals in the Ryan Center at the University of Rhode Island.

"Classical's beaten us twice," Nyblom continued, "but they can't play with us inside. Again, you have a lot of eyes on you. So let's go out there and show people how we play basketball. Let's show them how we take care of business under all kinds of scrutiny. This is what we've been practicing for all year. This is our moment."

Nyblom pointed to the three other coaches, and each one of them spoke. Jim Black told the team that there was still no respect for them around the state. Rob Whalen finished: "It took us three months to get here, but now we're here."

The Brown gym was packed. This was a gathering of the Rhode Island basketball community: the other high school coaches, the people who follow high school basketball without actually going to many games, the ones who keep the game alive year after year. So there was a sense of importance hanging over this game. And from the beginning Hope was ready for the challenge, not intimidated, as if this were just another game against a familiar team. But once again their flaws—their often poor foul shooting and their carelessness with the ball—were their biggest obstacles. Still, they played with great energy, great passion, and when they played like that they were a team no one wanted to play, as though their energy became their biggest weapon.

"Fellas, we stunk and we're up three," Nyblom said, back in the small locker room with pale walls and red lockers. "I don't even know how we're up. . . . Manny, don't try to do too much. Let the game come to you."

"Prove everyone wrong," said Jim Black. "Prove us right."

They came out in the second half like Teddy Roosevelt storming up San Juan Hill, their defense tenacious. And in the early minutes Classical succumbed to it. With just seven minutes left to play Hope was up thirteen, seemingly in command. But it wasn't going to be easy to finish the game out. The first game at Classical had gone to the final minute. The second game at Hope had been hotly contested to the final minutes. This figured to be similar.

But this time Classical was unable to stop Manny from getting to the rim; once again, as he'd done so many times during the season, he became Hope's offense. When Classical couldn't stop him, they fouled him. He kept going to the foul line and making his free throws. With just twenty seconds remaining in the game, Wayne made two huge free throws that gave Hope a six-point lead. It was enough of a cushion to win 69–65, and Hope became the Division I champions.

And when it was over, after the players had celebrated on the court in their big Hollywood moment, after the ceremony at center court was captured by television cameras from the three Providence TV stations, after a TV reporter interviewed Manny on the court, and after all the "Blue Wave" chants, there was Nyblom back in the joyous locker room. It all seemed so far away from the first home game of the season against North Kingstown, back when Manny and Delonce hadn't played in the first half, and everyone had been awful, and Hope had been embarrassed, and the season promised disaster.

Throughout the season Nyblom had repeatedly told his team that they were as good as any team in the state. That had been the endless mantra, over and over, from the day practice had started back in the gloom of late November, and now he felt a certain vindication. So he stood in the middle of the small locker room in a dark blue short-sleeve shirt and tan slacks, Nyblom's version of dressing up. Around him were both his jubilant team and a small cadre of the alumni, his ex-players who now had become, in their own way, his acolytes.

"Keep Hope alive!" yelled out Luis Ferreira, called "Captain Lou," in honor of being the last official captain Nyblom had named—and that had been five years ago. Nyblom believed that being a captain was an honor, not something ceremonial, and that it should go to someone who exhibited real leadership skills. Since "Captain Lou," he had never found one.

"ONE, TWO, THREE, HOPE!" yelled out the players.

Into the room came a jubilant Marquis Young.

"Didn't I see you quit a month ago?" asked Rob Whelan.

Marquis laughed.

Then into the room strode Manny.

"Yo, yo, no more interviews," he called out, as if he were Michael Jordan.

"I didn't have the courage to tell the other guys to shut up," he said, while Delonce went around the room and shook all the coaches' hands.

"If we had lost there would have been no more practices," he said, as if he had seen a chilling vision, a sneak preview of the future in the alumni in the room, guys who had left a piece of themselves in similar locker rooms in past years and now came in to wish the current players congratulations, in words that were etched with both envy and regret.

"Come on," Nyblom said, "we've got a long bus ride home."

Delonce Wright was sitting in the gym the next afternoon waiting for practice to start and talking about his Spanish class, specifically that he was failing it. It was another gray afternoon, the light coming in through the windows.

"If I didn't have Spanish I'd be on the honor roll," he said.

"Can you say a sentence in Spanish?" I asked him.

"Nope," he said with a smile. "Nothing. I don't know anything. A whole group of us don't know anything. I've got an F in Spanish and if I didn't have that I'd be on the honor roll. The teacher thinks that if you're in Spanish III you're supposed to know Spanish, but a lot of us don't. There's like twenty kids in the class and only about seven can speak it."

Why was this?

He said he had taken Spanish I when he'd been a freshman at St. Andrew's, but then didn't take it when he started at Hope as a sophomore.

"Last year in Spanish II we didn't do much," he said.

He shrugged. Life in the inner city.

Then he started talking about the season, about how they are finally now becoming a team, about how everything has changed, and about how he knows he's in the middle of something he'll never forget.

"I know I'm going to remember this forever."

The clock was winding down on his high school basketball career, one way or the other. And it was as though he sensed that never again would he be with his teammates in the same way, that a season ending was like a little death, changing everything, even if he wasn't ready for the change.

But there was no question that everything had been heightened.

There also was no question that Hope was in the middle of the spotlight, courtesy of the realities of the state tournament and the legacy of their well-publicized fight with La Salle, a fact of life Nyblom addressed once again the next afternoon back in the gym as all the players sat in the circle at half court. Their next game would be in the first round of the state championship, to be played at CCRI in Warwick. Their opponent would be Coventry, a team they had lost to earlier in the season.

"The Negroes have been acting up again," he said. "Starting fights. Using ineligible players. Acting like punks."

He paused.

"I'm so sick of picking up the paper and reading about all the thugs from the East Side, and all the Negroes who are terrifying everybody, and you should be too."

The players were silent.

"Have any of you thanked your teachers for coming to your games?" he asked.

Five kids raised their hands.

"Have any of you thanked Coach Moors? He brings you T-shirts. He gets us the disc jockey. He does all of this out of his own pocket. Do you ever say thank you?"

He gave them a long stare, an edge in his voice.

"Do you ever say thank you to Coach Whalen and Coach Black, who come here every day and volunteer their time for you? Because they don't get paid either. Do you ever say thank you to the people in the school who help you? Or your parents, who are trying to put food on the table for you? Or your teachers, who are trying to help you?"

He paused for a second, stared at them, and when he spoke again his voice was softer.

"Do you ever say thank you for anything?"

They were still sitting on the floor a few minutes later when Jerry Morgan walked in and gave Nyblom a big hug. He is in his seventies now, a tall thin black man in a dark suit. Once he was Nyblom's mentor, the Hope coach who gave him a chance to be a volunteer coach when Nyblom first began at Hope as a gym teacher in 1985.

Morgan first came to Providence in the early '60s to try out for the Boston Patriots, now the New England Patriots, then playing in the old American Football League. He had grown up in Gary, Indiana, coming of age in the '50s in a grim steel town, but to him there had been leagues to play in and people in the community who had cared for him.

"And there were no drugs and no guns," he said simply.

The practice was ragged and edgy, as if one from a couple of weeks ago had been recycled.

"Forty-year-old point guard!" Moors yelled out at Wayne, who clearly was doing little more than going through the motions, as if his personal goal were to expend as little energy as possible. "Forty-year-old point guard."

Wayne seemed oblivious.

Once again Moors was keeping up a running commentary during the practice:

"TURNOVER."

"CAN'T MAKE A LAYUP."

"BIG-SHOT BOB."

"MOUSE IN THE HOUSE."

All said with Moors's soft smile.

"We lose tomorrow, we go home, fellas!" Nyblom yelled out. "Play like this tomorrow, and this is the last practice."

"TURNOVER!" Moors yelled out. "Forty-year-old point guard, and silly sophomores."

A few of the jayvee kids were now practicing with the varsity, since their season was over. One of them, J.J., a thin black kid, was sulking in the corner.

"What's his problem?" someone asked Moors.

"Gangnam Style," he said, a reference to one of the hottest rap songs in the country. "Who knows?"

"Hey, Delonce," Moors said. "What color socks tomorrow night?"

"Ain't gone shopping yet," Delonce shot back.

It had already become a wasted practice when Manny and Johnson got into a verbal squabble over something no one could figure out and Nyblom told them to all go home.

"East Side punks. East Side thugs," Nyblom said with a smile, after the players had left. "Certainly seemed so today."

CHAPTER SEVENTEEN

Hendricken and La Salle were playing in the first game at CCRI in Warwick when Hope arrived and went into the CCRI locker room, which turned out to be appreciably bigger than the one they had been assigned the last time they were here.

"No pregame movies in here?" Moors asked.

"No," said Delonce. "We're cool."

Angel Rivera sat in a large chair that looked as if it belonged in someone's TV room. Wayne lay on the floor in the back of the room with headphones on. A few minutes later Nyblom walked in.

"Are we ready, gentlemen?" he said. "There's a good crowd out there and let's show them we're the best team in the state."

You could hear the cheers from the first game of the double-header, Hendricken and La Salle, as Nyblom told them that they had to run and they had to push the ball against Coventry. It was his ongoing message, for he knew that running the court was the only way his team could win. If he had harbored any illusions in the beginning of the year that this team could be successful by controlling tempo and beating teams in the half court, he now accepted reality.

Wayne was still lying in the back of the room out of Nyblom's sight, headphones on, slowly moving his head back and forth to a musical beat only he could hear. Somehow it seemed symbolic.

"Who are we going to get the ball to?" he asked.

"Wayne," came a voice.

"That's right," Nyblom said. "The little guy with the yellow socks and the ugly orange sneakers."

He looked around, as if trying to see where Wayne was, couldn't find him, and turned to Quenton Marrow.

"How many games we have to win before we're the state champions?" he asked.

"Four," said Marrow.

"Anyone else?" he asked the coaches.

"Me and Mr. Kargbo are on the same page," said Jim Black.

"Yeah, but different notebook," Manny shot back.

"Anyone?" Nyblom asked the players.

"We're good, yo," Johnson Weah said.

"Let's do this for all the people who supported you, and all the others who didn't believe in you," Moors said.

In the back of the room Wayne was now lying down with a black coat over his face.

"Pregame jitters," Rob Whalen whispered to me with a laugh.

But if they weren't visibly nervous they still started the game with three straight turnovers, and as the first half went on Manny looked tired and worn out, taking deep breaths during time outs, his weakened state arguably the main reason they were back in the locker room down one at the half.

Manny sat hunched over in the locker room.

"He's sick," Nyblom said. "Someone else is going to have to pick us up."

He glanced at the first-half stat sheet.

"Right now we're looking to make excuses," he continued. "All this is, fellas, is a lack of effort and a rotten practice yesterday. And I don't see one guy who is pissed. Not one. And I don't see anyone with good energy. What I do see is a lot of guys just waiting to get beat. And right now I don't like what I see. Because right now this looks like a bunch of guys who look defeated."

He looked at the other coaches, then turned back to the players.

"We can't do it for you." he said, his voice louder now. "You have to do it."

He turned and nodded to Luis Ferreira, "Captain Lou." Nyblom was a great believer in his players hearing different voices, that it couldn't always be him trying to push them, motivate them, couldn't always be his voice.

"Show some fuckin' pride!" Ferreira hollered. "THIS IS BULLSHIT. I believe in you. You have to believe in yourselves. Wake the fuck up. Show some pride. You aren't defeated yet."

His intensity was all over his face as he glared at the players.

"WAKE THE FUCK UP!" he yelled again.

It was a tie game to play with thirteen minutes left.

"Show them you're the best player in the state," Moors said to Manny during a time out. "We know you're sick. Fight through it."

With just 3:36 left they were down four. But Manny scored in the lane and now it was a two-point game. And as the pressure turned up and Coventry refused to go away, it was Manny's uncanny ability to get to the rim that was keeping Hope's season alive; it was as if he were somehow playing downhill. It was

what I had first seen that afternoon back in Charlestown, back
when he had seemed able to get to the rim almost at will once
the game opened up, like a Rhode Island version of Dwyane
Wade. When he got to the rim and scored it was as if everyone else fed off him. Then Wayne made a big shot from the left
side and Eli Lewis scored on a break with just twenty-nine seconds
left and the game was tied. Then, in the last seconds, Manny
drove to the basket, got fouled, and with the CCRI gym in an
uproar, in one of those moments right out of a Hollywood movie,
he made two free throws. Seven seconds later Hope was moving
on to the quarterfinals of the state tournament.

It was the next afternoon, before practice, and Wayne Clements
sat in the front row of the bleachers watching Angel Rivera
shooting at the far basket. Nyblom pushed a broom up and down
the court.

"Follow through, my son," Wayne said, as if he were a wiz-
ened old player, now in his twilight years, trying to impart hard-
earned wisdom to the next generation.

It somehow seemed fitting. For there was little question that
Wayne had long ago checked out emotionally, if not physically.
He now seemed to move to some private rhythm only he could
understand, carrying some sadness with him. His behavior in
the locker room before the last game had been so over the top,
so bizarre, that he had been fortunate Nyblom hadn't seen it.
Neither Nyblom, nor anyone else, seemed able to reach him in
any significant way.

And the irony was that he wasn't difficult. He didn't talk
back to the coaches. He didn't argue with his teammates. He was
by no means a selfish player. Nor was he any kind of troublemaker. In many ways he was the team's most valuable player,
for his presence alone made Hope a much better team. What he
gave them—stability, leading a team on the floor, understanding

how to play, consistently making perimeter shots—no one else could. When he had begun playing, Hope's season had started turning around, and without him Hope would not have made the playoffs.

Yet he'd become the textbook definition of disengaged.

And now he sat in the front row of the bleachers like a life-guard on a beach, the one who sees everything from behind dark glasses, and who no one ever really sees.

He pointed at Eli Lewis.

"That's my other son," he said. "I have two sons here."

Then he said something to Angel, who yelled back, "I can't hear you."

Wayne pointed to his head.

Then he pointed to Eli.

"Yo, my son, go over there like Nyblom said."

He was wearing a black-and-gray Raiders beanie, light jeans with holes in them, and a gray sweatshirt. He was not practic-ing, resting both his balky knee and a sore right hand.

"Keep that dribble low, girl," he said to Eli. "Stop carrying the ball."

"Work harder, my son," he said to Angel.

Then it was back to Eli.

"Keep your head up, my son. How can you be my son with no handle?"

He peered off in the direction of the large Palladian windows across the court, as if looking at something only he could see.

"Every time I play I get better," he said, "and I never sat on a bench in my life. And I'm never afraid. Because I know what's coming."

This was said with no obvious braggadocio, simply a state-ment of fact. As it is when he says he never gets nervous before games, because it's just another game, and hadn't he already played in a zillion of them, ever since he was a little kid in South

Providence at the Sackett Street rec center where his father worked?

He grew up with the game, and he was a student of it.

"I taught myself by watching other people play," he said. "My father gave me the basics, but I was always watching guys."

"Like who?" I asked.

"Allen Iverson. LeBron. Isiah Thompson."

"Thomas," I said.

"Oh yeah, Isiah Thomas."

He paused for a second, as if lost in thought.

"Hey, Showtime," Nyblom yelled over to him. "You practicing today?"

"Forty-year-old point guard," Moors said loudly.

But the tone had changed. For if everyone understood that they couldn't win without Wayne, they also had come to know that they weren't going to change him, either. Not in the quarterfinals of the state tournament, where success depended on getting the ball in Wayne's hands while overlooking his trespasses (if not exactly forgiving them).

"My hand hurts," he said softly. "I don't know if I can even get any shots up today."

But then in the next moment he began telling me that he had been throwing empty juice bottles at Ben's window at 6:30 in the morning because they had been planning to go to Foot Locker in the Providence Place Mall to buy new sneakers.

"They can't win without you, you know," I said, looking out at his teammates, who were now warming up.

"I know," he said. "I saw it at the beginning of the year. It wasn't pretty."

He said his plan was to go to CCRI—what he referred to as "CeeCee"—where he says he will have a different attitude.

"I'll have a new start there. Play like I really want to play. Because right now I don't really care. This team frustrates me."

He paused, looked out onto the court, the start of another practice.

"I lost my love of the game in my freshman year. I didn't like all the arguing. And the ball should be moving around me. Because I'll pass it to them. But guys are selfish."

I pointed to the Raiders beanie on his head.

"So you like the Raiders?' I asked.

"Nah, not really," he said. "I just like the hat."

"Okay, Cupcake," Nyblom said, calling over to Wayne. "Let's go."

CHAPTER EIGHTEEN

It was Sunday noon and the Hope players were in a cramped locker room inside Alumni Hall on the Providence College campus, the Catholic school in the north end of the city, which is about a jump shot away from La Salle to the southwest and the Chad Brown housing project to the southeast. The school has been there since 1919, back when it was a small, mostly commuter college that once had been described as a place for "poor Catholic kids" to go. Then, in the late '50s, with a new gym and a young coach named Joe Mullaney, who later would go on to coach the Lakers, the Friars would come out of nowhere to win the then-prestigious National Invitational Tournament in New York and begin a basketball story that is legendary to this day: two trips to the Final Four, the Big East Conference, a basketball program that has used Alumni Hall as a practice gym for forty years now.

But if the Friars had been playing their games in a downtown arena ever since Richard Nixon was in the White House, Alumni Hall was a clean, refurbished campus gym that could seat nearly three thousand people. To the Hope kids it was the big-time, far away from their small, old gym on the second floor of Hope. It was also an obvious example that their season had now gone uptown, beyond the often insular world of the Rhode Island Interscholastic League, complete with the increased media attention that came with such a stage.

They were about to play Hendricken, the same team they had lost to in the first league game of the season back in early December, the same Hendricken team they hadn't beaten in six years.

"I think we're something like 0-9 against them," Moors said. "Maybe it's worse than that."

The day before, there had been a cookout at Nyblom's house in South Kingstown, the message being that the Hope basketball team was more than just the practice and the games, but something larger, too. While sometimes lost on his players, this message meant that these young men were a part of something, that which had come before and that which would follow, Nyblom always referencing the alumni, even if the alumni too often seemed to consist of a few former players who hung around once in a while. In many ways this was the hardest message to send in a big urban high school that often seemed so removed from everything around it, even its past.

When he spoke to the team, Nyblom really did seem like a contemporary "White Shadow," walking on the tightrope between tough love and the catcher in the rye, trying to keep his kids from going off the cliff.

"Someone said the KKK lived around here," Moors went on. "It was hilarious. Johnson and Angel missed the bus in Providence, and Dave's wife, who was in the city, picked them up and brought them down. She got Johnson downtown in Kennedy Plaza, where the buses are, and then they had to go to Chad Brown to get Angel, and when she finally got onto Branch

Avenue she asked, 'Is it safe now?' The whole night was great. Video games. A lot of laughing and joking around. Great Team Building."

Devante Youn was in a dark suit, having just come from church.

As the players finished getting their uniforms on, into the locker room came Providence College basketball coach Ed Cooley, a big, burly black man. He was talking on a cell phone. Then he snapped it shut and stared at the players sitting in front of him.

"I was just talking to the father of one of the top recruits in the country," Cooley said loudly. "But the hell with him. He can wait. Because we're family."

Yes, they were. Not only is Cooley the first African-American coach in Providence College's long basketball history, he grew up in South Providence and had had a childhood that could have come out of a Dickens novel—eating cereal with water, going to a school in what he calls "bummy clothes" because there was no money, and spending a lot of time as an adolescent living in his friend's house because his mother couldn't always take care of him. Cooley was them. Same city. Same neighborhood. Same high school league. Same obstacles. Same dreams. He had parlayed being an All Stater at Central into a year at a New England prep school and a scholarship to Stonehill, a Division II school in southeastern Massachusetts. He had been a high school teacher, before he walked away at twenty-seven years old to become a graduate assistant at the University of Rhode Island, learning the college coaching profession from the ground up, paying his dues for years. All those dues and all those years finally led him back home to this dream job, a high-paid Big East coaching position in his hometown. He was now standing in front of this Hope team as a living example that dreams can indeed come true, if you only do the right thing.

"Go out there and play as hard as you can for as long as you can," he said in his deep voice.

"One game away from going back to the Ryan Center," said Moors after Cooley had left the room.

A few minutes later they came out onto the varnished court in their white T-shirts with "Refuse to Lose" in big letters on the front, and "A.F.P." in blue letters on the right sleeve. There was a large crowd, with a media table at courtside, and TV cameramen and photographers. They wore their dark blue uniforms with gold-and-white trim, Hendricken white uniforms with green-and-gold trim.

But if the setting was different from the first time these two teams had played each other back in early December, and the stakes were certainly different, the first half was remarkable similar. Once again the game was physical, intense. Once again Hope had trouble scoring. Once again it was a slow, half-court game, the kind of game Hope had struggled with all year. Once again Hope found themselves trailing at halftime, down 22-17.

"Fellas, they're beating you at their game," Nyblom said when they were back in the small locker room. His voice was soft, his tone comforting. "We can't beat them at their game. We have to play our game. We have to push the ball and speed the pace up. Hey, we stunk and we're only chasing five points. But if we keep playing at this pace we're going to lose."

"Sixteen minutes to the Ryan Center," Moors said. "This is your season right here."

They listened.

As soon as the second half began Hope sped up the pace. They played defense in a frenzy, with a sense of urgency that had been missing in the first half. With ten minutes left to play they were leading by four. Not that Hendricken was going to go away easily. They had too much pride, too much tradition, and they were too well coached to do that. Hendricken was a team used to playing tournament games, and their players were used to winning them. That was their tradition, and both the coaches and the players seemed to carry it with them like a signboard. They were Hendricken, and they were supposed to win games like this. They were Hendricken, and the green-and-gold banners on their gym walls back in Warwick were proof that they won games like this. So it was no surprise when they fought back and went up by one with seven and a half minutes left to play.

But Wayne countered with a three-pointer, and once again Hope had the lead.

Two and a half minutes later, thanks to another Wayne Clements three-point shot, Hope was leading 46-38. There was a shade over three minutes left to play. Were they going to do it again, come out of the scrap heap like they'd done the year before and get back to the state semifinals at the Ryan Center at the University of Rhode Island?

Not so fast.

A minute later Hendricken had cut the lead to two, and two Hope turnovers later they were up 47-46 with just 1:28 left to play. Was this going to be like the first game of the season, the one at Hendricken, where Hope had lost an ugly scrum of a game the same way, ground down by Hendricken's gritty defense? Had it all come down to this, all the practices and all the bus rides, a mirror image of the first game of the year?

Hope came down the court, Wayne missed a shot, and Hendricken called a time out with just fifty-eight seconds to play. Alumni Hall was bedlam. This was high school playoff basketball at its best, two teams in the last minute, both fighting to get into the state semifinals at the University of Rhode Island.

Hendricken put the ball in play, obviously trying to run down the shot clock as long as they could without taking a shot. Will Tavares, the Hawks' leading scorer, was out near half court, trying to milk the clock, all the while being hounded by

Delonce Wright. But he held the ball too long, was called for a five-second violation that gave the ball back to Hope.

Hope raced down the court in the pandemonium the gym had become, the clock ticking down, and Ben Vezele took a hurried shot from the corner that missed.

Enter the basketball gods.

The ball bounced into the hands of Wayne Clements, who flicked it off the glass backboard and through the hoop with just thirteen seconds remaining and Hope now leading 48-47.

Hendricken came quickly back down the court, Alumni Hall in an uproar, but a baseline shot from the Hawks' Ryan Hagerty was blocked out of bounds by Johnson Weah.

There were now 4.5 seconds remaining.

Hendricken took a time out.

They got the ball to senior Kazre Cummings, who shot a quick three-pointer from the top of the circle, and in the ensuing melee it bounced out to Hagerty on the left. He flipped the ball in one motion, and the ball somehow went in, only to be ruled too late, as the buzzer ending the game had already sounded.

Hope was going to the state semifinals.

There was pandemonium on the court, the players jumping around in wild celebration, people cheering, Manny and Delonce posing for pictures, other people hugging the players, all the fruits of victory right there in full display. It all seemed so far from the first league game of the season at Hendricken when they had been so offensively inept, so lost, like a team that had met for the first time outside in the parking lot five minutes before the game started.

"It's never pretty and it's never easy," said Rob Whalen, shaking his head in a big grin. "We just somehow find a way to win."

Several minutes later, back in the joyous locker room, Nyblom called it a great victory for Hope.

"This was for the teachers, students, alumni, everybody," he said. "So tomorrow in school thank everyone you see. And you guys on the bench. Cheering. Supporting everyone. You were great. That's what this is all about. A great team victory."

If all happy families are alike, as Tolstoy once said, so are all happy teams.

Or as Delonce Wright said, "We went from stealing basketballs to stealing championships. The greatest two years ever."

Three days later Nyblom was pushing a broom up the old court in his tan shorts, blue short-sleeve shirt, and white sneakers. It was very hot in the gym, like a sauna.

"Manny, you getting dressed today or not?" he asked, an edge in his voice.

In many ways practice had become little more than filler between the glamour of the games. It was inevitable. There had been so many of them. For here it was the first week of March, the bitter cold seemingly over, the light outside different, the New England gloom that William Faulkner had once called "the iron dark" starting to change. They had been in this gym virtually every afternoon since the last few days of November, and practice held no more surprises. Their roles on the team had long been established. They didn't need to get in better shape. They were on a great run and they wanted to keep playing big games in front of big crowds, the sooner the better. The last thing they wanted was another practice against the same faces, another afternoon of having to play hard while Nyblom and the other coaches watched them with jewelers' eyes.

The day before, practice had been light, little more than going through the motions. There had been a camera crew from Cox—a local network that did a lot of sports—which was going to televise the semifinals and finals from the Ryan Center at the University of Rhode Island, and the four senior starters had been put on camera, saying their name and stating that they play for "The Blue Wave," a little sliver of the big-time right here in this old gym on the second floor of Hope. It had been one of those fantasy moments and the four seniors had had fun with it, especially Manny, who fumbled his one line and laughed. One more reminder that winning changed everything, opened up the world.

But now it was the day before the semifinal game, the start of practice, and the vibe was different. So it shouldn't have been a surprise that after watching Manny take ten minutes or so to put on his sneakers and Wayne sprawled on the last row of the bleachers as if he were passed out on a downtown park bench, and everyone else doing little more than going through the motions, Nyblom put his game face on.

Eventually, they began some calisthenics at the center of the court, Quenton Marrow leading them. It was just the latest example that Quenton possessed innate leadership skills, even if he played sparingly. But the players were not focused, and Nyblom had had enough.

"The last I knew I'm still the coach here and it's 3:45 and we haven't done a damn thing yet, so start running."

They started doing laps around the gym, Quenton the only one taking it seriously, his long strides making him look like the track athlete he was in the spring. None of the four seniors really wanted to be leaders—or, maybe more important, didn't understand what it meant to be a leader; even now at the end of the season, each was too self-absorbed to do anything more than give lip service to the very idea of leadership. Manny was too moody, even if on the court both his talent and his will to win could seem like leadership. Johnson was too proud to put himself in that kind of role, self-conscious about his language skills, as if at some level he still carried the baggage of his Liberian childhood. Delonce was more of an observer by nature. And

Wayne? Wayne was the great enigma, a leader on the court with the ball in his hands, disengaged off it.

Now they were all just part of the pack, jogging around the court's perimeter. Somehow it seemed symbolic.

"Come on, Manny!" yelled Jim Black. "You should be leading the way."

Manny continued jogging in the middle of the pack.

"Hey, J.J.!" Black yelled to the sophomore who had been brought up to the varsity now that the junior varsity season was over. "If you're going to have an attitude, go home. We didn't need you in the regular season and we don't need you now."

Manny continued to jog in the middle of the pack, expressionless, as if lost in some private rhythm.

"Go home, Superstar," Nyblom yelled, the bite in his voice. "If you're not going to work, just go home."

"You're a dog, and you're lazy," Nyblom called out to Eli Lewis. "You could be great, but you're a dog."

They kept jogging around the gym until Nyblom brought them to the circle at center court, where they sat down.

"You act like we've already won," he said. "But right now our practice methods suck. So leave the gym. Go out in the hall and wait until I come get you."

Manny walked over to the bleachers and picked up his cell phone.

"Leave the phone and get out."

Ten minutes later Nyblom called them back in.

"Gentlemen, nothing in life is a given. You've got to earn it. You had something good going on here, but now it's over."

He pointed to two boxes on the side of the court.

"There are five pairs of shorts in that box, and there are thirteen pairs of shirts in that box. Coach Moors bought them with his own money. They better be here tomorrow, or we run again tomorrow. That's your call."

"Maybe we can actually look like a team," Moors said.

"And each of you has to shut your mouth," Nyblom said, pointing to Wayne. "There's the door. If you don't like what we're doing and you want to go home, go."

Then he pointed at Eli Lewis.

"You haven't practiced hard all year, Eli, and now you've been loafing all day."

Pedro Correia stood nearby, a disgusted look on his face. "Don't cry when you lose Friday night," he said.

They began a full-court defensive drill, but it didn't take Nyblom long to tell Eli Lewis to go sit down. Then when Eli took his shirt off and threw it on the floor Nyblom told him to leave the gym and start running up and down the long hallway that went from the gym to the front of the school on one side of the courtyard.

"In ten minutes or so I'm going to come out. If I see you running the hallway hard maybe you can come back in. That's maybe," Nyblom said loudly to Eli. "But you better be running hard."

A half hour later the players were back in the circle at half court, sitting down while Nyblom and the other coaches stood in front of them.

"If you all worked as hard as this kid," he said, pointing to Johnson Weah, "we'd be undefeated. That kid plays defense every day for no glory. He doesn't ask for anything. He doesn't expect anything. He doesn't question anything. He just brings it every day."

He looked away, then back to his team.

"The games should be easy compared to our practices. Instead we have to put up with bullshit after bullshit."

He pointed to Eli, shook his head.

"This kid has all the talent in the world, but he's his own worst enemy."

He paused, and when he spoke again, his voice was softer, the edge gone.

"Wouldn't it be nice to just have a good practice? If we did that we would roll over teams. The games would be easy. Instead, we loaf and have attitudes. We're our own worst enemy."

He again pointed to Eli.

"But this kid has a terrible attitude, and Devante is lazy, and Wayne is the worst kind of dog."

The players sat silent on the floor.

"These coaches are volunteers," he continued, motioning toward Moors, Rob Whalen, and Jim Black. "They don't get paid and they spend all kinds of their own money on you. Do you appreciate it? Do you ever tell them you appreciate it?"

He looked away, the disgust all over his face.

"But you're still lazy," he continued, looking back at them. "We blow off practice like it doesn't count, but we're only two games away from being the state champions. Why?"

He pointed at Manny.

"Because Mr. Miserable over here can get to the rim better than anyone in the state, and when the lights go on you all come to play. I can't coach that. Nobody can. You guys do that, and you should be proud of yourselves."

CHAPTER NINETEEN

On March 8, two yellow school buses were outside in the parking lot, and Keith Moors stood inside the cramped coach's office, where the clock on the wall still said 6:32.

"They had a little thing for the players at URI this morning," he said. "The room was packed. They had principals and athletic directors and players from all the teams there. None of our kids talked. They were all scared to death to talk.

"But I'm nervous. North Kingstown is the one team I didn't want to see. They're a good team, big and strong and experienced. They play well together. This is the worst matchup for us."

One bus was the fan bus, the first time there had been one all season. But there were still no cheerleaders. A few years before, they had started out with twenty-five girl cheerleaders and ended up with six after endless feuds and personality clashes, and the cheerleading program was finally just dropped.

The buses went out of the parking lot and took a left on Hope Street. Most of the players had headsets on. Nyblom went down the aisle passing out candy bars. There would be no food before the game.

"What you do?" Moors asked. "Rob a candy store?"

The bus was soon stuck in traffic, with downtown off to the left and the West End off to the right. It was a dreary, foggy afternoon, with flakes of snow that didn't stick. The ride took about an hour, as the traffic was heavy going to the southern Rhode Island suburbs, the bus passing through Warwick, East Greenwich, and North Kingstown before heading into South Kingstown and the University of Rhode Island.

The bus drove through the north end of the campus to the Ryan Center, a close-to-eight-thousand-seat arena, and the players went into one of the small locker rooms on the ground floor of the building. Wayne wore a white towel over his head.

"Forty-year-old point guard," laughed Moors.

The game was an hour away.

Everyone was getting dressed except Wayne, and a song by Drake was all but bouncing off the walls.

"Started from the bottom now we're here, nigga . . . Started from the bottom and the whole team fucking here."

Rap had become the soundtrack to a generation, of course, both the celebration of the street and the commercialization of it.

Wayne put on blue socks, orange sneakers, and a big gray hooded sweatshirt over his blue uniform.

"Hey, Wayne," Nyblom said as he walked into the locker room. "We put in a waiver so you can play with your hoodie on."

Wayne took the hoodie off, only to reveal his black-and-gray Raiders hat.

"SSDD," Nyblom laughed as he turned away. "Same shit, different day."

The Drake song continued, "Nigga started from the bottom now we're here."

"I can't stand it," Pedro Correia said to me in the corner of the locker room. "I'm sixty years old. I know what that word meant. I was very angry in my younger years when kids began to use it, and I tried to explain to them what the word meant historically, but so much of that has been lost. They just don't understand it."

He looked out over the locker room as the song continued.

"We've made a ton of mistakes as a society," he continued, "but this one can't be justified. These kids don't have a clue to what that word meant. The media should be ashamed. They're selling these kids out."

He paused, then spoke again, his words marked by pain and regret.

"I try not to overreact. But it burns me inside."

He paused again, looked away, as if seeing something only he could see, then turned back and looked at the kids in the locker room, kids who reminded him of what he had once been like, a kid of color trying to figure out where he fit in the world, although he knew it was more difficult now, too many families under attack, too many neighborhoods under siege. "But you know what? You can't not keep rooting for these kids. Because they have so many odds against them."

Seven blue-and-white NCAA banners hung from the rafters of the Ryan Center, a large arena with dark blue seats. On this night a couple thousand people filled them, most from North Kingstown, a big suburban school in the neighboring town. It was the same North Kingstown team that had tattooed Hope back in their first home league game of the regular season, a night when Wayne didn't play and Manny had been held out for the first half because he was being punished. Hope had been in complete disarray, and I had wondered about what I had signed up for, if following the Hope basketball team through a season would be worthwhile. They had come so far from that night of dysfunction and turmoil, when the state tournament seemed about as far away as some distant star in the nighttime sky.

North Kingstown was a good veteran team. This game would test Hope to its limits.

Hope warmed up for about fifteen minutes before coming back to the locker room, where Nyblom stood in the middle of the team.

"Let's relax and have some fun," he said. "There's no reason to be nervous. This is basketball, gentlemen. And keep your mouth shut with the referees. Your job is to play basketball, and just keep doing what you've been doing."

"We can't lose here two years in a row," said Delonce Wright. "We didn't come here for nothing. This is our time."

The coaches left the room and once again someone played the song by Drake, the new Hope anthem: "Started from the bottom now we're here, nigga . . . Started from the bottom and the whole team fucking here."

Once again they went out of the locker room wearing their white "Refuse to Lose" T-shirts over their uniforms, "A.F.P." on the sides.

Went out to move one step closer to a state championship.

After the first few minutes they were leading 14-6, off to a great start. Only a few thousand people were in the arena, but its size and the importance of the game were a different reality from Hope's little old gym on the second floor, the one that seemed stuck in some gone-forever decade. And unlike the game the two teams had played back at Hope in mid-December, when it was clear from the beginning that the veteran North Kingstown team was far superior, now the two teams seemed evenly matched, a tribute to how far Hope had come. Still, there were stylistic differences. North Kingston wanted to run their half-court offensive sets, basketball out of a textbook, even if the textbook had been upgraded to suit the times. Hope wanted to push the pace, use their athleticism to both pressure North Kingstown and create space where they could get to the rim before North Kingstown had a chance to set up defensively. This was the chess match, the game within the game.

With just under seven minutes left in the half Hope was down 15-14, a snapshot of how the game was going to play out. For, in truth, there was little difference between the two teams, save for their different philosophies. They both played with great intensity. And they both knew that if they lost their season was over, just like that, so they played with a sense of frenetic urgency, too. At the half Hope was down 28-24, once again hurt by the combination of their poor perimeter shooting and their struggles to finish at the rim.

"We took their best punch and we're only down four," said Moors as they came into the locker room. "So my halftime speech is real simple: make your layups."

Nyblom pounded the same theme.

"Right now we're sloppy and unfocused. We look nervous and we shouldn't be. We've been here before and they haven't. Look, gentlemen, we stunk and we're only chasing four."

He clapped his hands.

"Heart will lead us," he said, his voice rising. "Hope on three."

The players came together in a circle in the middle of the room, their hands touching as they held them high over their heads.

"ONE, TWO, THREE, HOPE!" they yelled.

For they still believed. Hadn't they been in this same situation so many times before? Hadn't this been the story of their season: getting off to poor starts, falling behind, and having to play catch-up? Hadn't they always felt as if they were running up a mountain, as if the game had become symbolic of their lives, behind and trying to catch up, always trying to overcome the odds?

They quickly went down seven in the early minutes of the second half. Then Wayne hit two three-point shots to give them a one-point lead. But for all of their passion and all of their energy, they couldn't hold the lead. North Kingstown kept running an effective offense, while they, in turn, were hurt by the same weaknesses that had been there since the season had started. With 6:10 left to play Hope was again trailing, by ten points, the scoreboard clock counting down the minutes of their season.

But then Manny scored on two drives to the basket, once again showing that he could get to the basket against anyone. So now, with five and a half minutes left in the game, they were only down five. But Johnson had four fouls and time was slipping away, precious seconds disappearing off the clock.

When Ben scored in the lane with 3:40 left Hope was only down three, still breathing, still alive, as if their season suddenly had found one more life. And in the last hectic minutes the tension rose, with a bigger crowd now, as more people had come for the second game of the doubleheader, Hope fighting for its season to continue.

With thirty-three seconds left in the game North Kingstown was leading 56–50 after a Chris Hess layup. They now appeared to be in control. But then Johnson Weah, who rarely ever took a three-point shot, made one with just 12.9 seconds left in the game. North Kingstown's Hess then missed the front end of a one-and-one free throw. Now there was a shade over eight seconds left, Hope down three and needing a basketball miracle.

They got it.

Manny hit a three-point shot from the left side that tied the game.

Overtime.

Somehow it seemed only fitting.

Once again Hope had survived just when all was lost, as if this game had become a metaphor for their season, finding another life when it seemed as if they were out of them.

Could they capitalize on their momentum in overtime? Could they grab this game? Could they save this season, this season that already had been saved so many times before?

But it wasn't to be.

Wayne had fouled out with two and a half minutes left in the game, so Hope entered the overtime undermanned. They quickly fell behind, so again they were trying to play catch-up, trying to overcome the odds. In the last minute, the seconds clicking off the scoreboard clock, Hope was down 66-61, in a frantic comeback attempt, in search of another little basketball miracle. But Manny's three-point shot with just eleven seconds left was too little, too late, Hope losing 66-64 in overtime.

Manny had finished with twenty-one points, fifteen in the second half. Wayne had finished with seventeen.

More important, they had finished their high school careers, as had Johnson Weah, Delonce Wright, and Aaron Lynch.

As they came back to the locker room Marquis Young put his arm around Manny, as if supporting him. Manny sat down on a bench and pulled his blue uniform top over his head. The room was silent.

You could hear music outside the door, yelling and screaming. One game had ended, another was about to begin. One dream had ended. Others were still alive.

Jerry Morgan, the former Hope coach, and Ralph Taylor, who went back decades with minority athletes in Providence and now works as a community relations specialist at Hope, came into the room. They went around the room, quietly consoling the players, shaking their hands.

"Nothing to be ashamed of," Taylor said. "Sometimes it's just the breaks of the game."

In many ways Taylor was old Providence, had come of age when the city's minority community had been much smaller, a time when he was just one phone call away from knowing whatever he had to know about anyone.

Nyblom walked into the middle of the room, began speaking in a low voice.

"It hurt last year and it hurts again this year. I was praying that the kids in this locker room that were here last year remembered how we felt then. We talked then about lifting, doing summer stuff. But it didn't happen. And we should be here again next year if we do the right thing. Pay attention to school. Do the right thing at home. Support each other. But right now, going forward, everyone has to start thinking, school, school, school."

Silence.

That, and the realization that it was over. All the practices. All the bus rides. All the afternoons after school in the Health Room. All the locker rooms in all the schools they had played at, and all the emotion. It was now suddenly over, already in the past tense, and with that came the knowledge, however unarticulated, that never again would they all be sitting together in the same way. For Manny Kargbo, Wayne Clements, Johnson Weah, and Delonce Wright were all alumni now, whether they realized it or not, no different from Shaq Jones and Shaun Hill, no different from Malieke Young and "Coach Lou," from Mookie and Wook and Kofo and all the others who still floated in and out of the gym, here one minute, gone the next, as if the Hope gym were still their little life raft in a swirling sea. That was the great unspoken reality, of course, of how fleeting it all is—a season, a high school career, all of it.

"Keep your head up," said Jerry Morgan, the old coach who

had spent so much of his life in locker rooms just like this one. "I'm very proud of you."

"So am I," said Pedro Correia, this kind man who perhaps knew Hope and the kids who played at Hope better than anyone else, knew so many of the mountains they had to climb. "I've got nothing but praise for you. You overcame a lot of odds."

And in the end it was Nyblom again, now in the role of trying to lift up his hurting team, this team that had come so close to getting back to the state finals, this team that he had pushed and prodded all season, this team that he had fought with and picked up, too; this team that now owned a piece of his heart, just like all the others he'd coached through the years. These players whom he will continue to help, just as he's helped so many of the others, letting them hang around the gym during practice, or trying to get them into school somewhere, or just being their advocate, their booster, their friend.

That was the thing too few people understood, all the ones asking him through the years why he kept coaching at Hope, why he kept coaching kids few people wanted to deal with anymore, these kids who when they walked downtown white people crossed the street to avoid, all these dark-skinned kids in their hoodies, the ones society didn't seem to have a place for anymore. Why did he keep doing it, season after season, year after year, starting at ground zero?

Why?

Now he stood in the center of this small locker room, minutes after the season had ended in overtime, in the cruelest of ways, the dream of winning a state championship in symbolic pieces all around them on the locker room floor.

"We love you guys," he said, the emotion in his voice. "We love you."

EPILOGUE

It was June 2014, fifteen months after that night in the Ryan Center, and once again Nyblom had to give a eulogy for one of his former players.

This time it was for Derek Knighton, who had died of leukemia. Five years earlier he had been shot in the parking lot of a Providence nightclub, hit by a bullet that had been fired into the car he was in at closing time. Who fired on him? Why was he shot? Was it just a random act of violence in a city that seemed to have more of it all the time? Or was this just one more deadly incident in a long-standing feud between the Browns and the Lassiters and their extended families, which have been at each other's throats now for decades, a litany of murder and violence in Providence for a quarter of a century, passed down through the generations like some malevolent heirloom?

How did it start?

No one seemed to know anymore.

Knighton, who was part of the Lassiter family, had been an All State player for Hope, described by Nyblom as "a tough kid, someone who came from nothing." He grew up in the city's embattled west side, and Nyblom remembers the beds in Knighton's apartment were on cinder blocks with a piece of plywood over them. He also remembers giving Knighton and his brother a ride home from Hope, and that when they were getting out of the car and a ten-year-old kid went riding by on a bicycle the two boys were so spooked they jumped into nearby bushes.

He was one of the former players who always kept in touch with Nyblom, even if much of his life was in the street.

"I knew he was carrying a gun," Nyblom said. "He said he needed it."

He paused.

"He was a real tough, streetwise kid. But every once in a while he would break down and start bawling, say how he wanted to have a mother and father around."

Hope's season had been over for six weeks or so when Nyblom heard of Knighton's death. The season had begun with a certain optimism even if Manny, Wayne, Delonce, and Johnson were gone. Manny was at the University of California at Riverside—shepherded there by Hope's first-year principal, Tamara Sterling, who knew someone there—even though Manny wasn't academically eligible to play basketball his first year. He had been around during Christmas break, coming to practice and a couple of games. He had been happy, smiling, as if the pressure and angst he had felt for so much of his senior year had lifted. Delonce was at Dean, a junior college in nearby Franklin, Massachusetts, although for some reason hadn't played either football or basketball. Still, he came to a few games, visited the locker room, one of the alumni.

Johnson would make an appearance every once in a while too. He attended the Community College of Rhode Island. He was on the basketball team, playing in the same gym where just a few months before two of his teammates had held up his jersey when he had been banned from the playoff game due to the fight at La Salle, back when Hope had been all over the news. Also on that team was Malieke Young, nephew of Laurence Young, another alumnus.

Even Wayne showed up every once in a while.

He had failed to graduate high school, but was making up some credits, the plan being to play the following year at Johnson & Wales, a Providence school that played a Division III basketball schedule. He seemed happier too, as if the pressure he had felt the year before was now gone.

Their occasional presence was a reaffirmation that there really was a Hope basketball family, as dysfunctional as it could sometimes seem. It's what the coaches had been telling me the year before. For now these four were no different from Mookie and Wook, and "Captain Lou," and all the others who were part of this big extended family that went back through the decades.

The new alumni.

This is what no one else saw, of course. It didn't show up in the record book. It wasn't in the *Providence Journal*, or on the local television stations. It never got trumpeted. In fact, there were people in his own building, teachers and administrators alike, who had no idea what Nyblom routinely did to push his kids into colleges, who essentially saw him as the big, burly guy who walked around in shorts all day.

And in June 2014 there were two other kids from the team I had followed the year before going off to college, as both Marquis Young and Devante Youn were headed to the University of Rhode Island in the fall, accepted into the school's Talent Development program, the one designed for promising minority students from the state.

And then there was Ben Vezele.

Two months earlier he was named to the All State team by the *Providence Journal*, one of the five best high school players in

Rhode Island. It had been a disappointing season for Hope, one that had ended just short of making the playoffs, but in many ways Vezele had come into his own. He had grown bigger, now about six-foot-four, more assertive, one step closer to the potential the coaches always saw in him. He had come so far from the year before, was less shy, to the point that on the June morning I was supposed to meet him in the small parking lot behind Hope and couldn't find him, he yelled out, "Hey, Reynolds, over here," from a nearby car. He never would have had the confidence to do that the year before.

He had graduated, and in the fall he would be going off to Wilbraham & Monson, a New England prep school that's been around since 1804, one of those leafy places that speak of old money and privilege, so far from Hope and his South Providence neighborhood.

"A year ago I didn't even know what a prep school was," he said.

He was sitting in the front seat of my car and saying how prep school was so important because it was his passport to college. And as he talked about it I thought of my conversation with his sister, Yasah, a few months earlier; how she remembered fleeing Liberia to a refugee camp, how "God had his hand on us," and how soon after they made their way to Rhode Island and this new life; how Ben had been the first boy after five sisters, and how she had called him "our answered prayer."

Now he was talking about how important college was to him, looking outside the car window for something only he could see, this inner-city kid on the morning after his high school graduation, this kid who knew all about his family's tortured history, this family that had seen things no one should ever see.

"My father is getting old, and I'm the only male," Vezele said softly. "So I have to one day become the leader of my family."

Vezele's going to prep school in the fall of 2014 also meant that there now would be seven kids from that team I had followed the season before continuing their education after Hope, an amazing figure for an inner-city high school team in Providence.

It was a testimony to several things, of course, not the least being the constant prodding from Nyblom and the other coaches, the message that there was a bigger world outside of the Hope gym, one that was open to them if they would only do the right things. Hadn't this been the message in all those after-practice sessions when they would sit at half court, when it so often seemed as if they were going to drown in the dysfunction swirling all around them? Hadn't this always been Nyblom's refrain, that the world could open up to them if only they would let it; that the world was full of opportunities and that you didn't have to be defined by your neighborhood, didn't have to be defined by other people's perceptions of you?

In many ways this was Nyblom's great gift, and it had nothing to do with all the x's and o's drawn on blackboards, nothing to do with wins and losses, nothing to do with all the obvious ways coaches are measured.

That, and his unwavering loyalty.

Year after year.

A couple of weeks later, one of the last days of the school year, Nyblom sat in the cramped little coach's office, the one that looked as if the calendar on the wall said 1958, and the clock still read 6:32. Two kids from the past season's jayvee team poked their heads into the office, wearing their youth as if it were some kind of merit badge. One looked out from a gray hoodie.

"Yo, Nyblom," the kid said. "When's summer league start?"

"I told you," Nyblom said, exasperated. "Two weeks. How many times I have to say it?"

"Yeah, yeah," the kid said. "But where it at?"

Nyblom turned away and shook his head. Then he laughed.

Another season was about to begin.

In September of 2015, Quenton Marrow was shot three times in what appeared to be a random act of violence, shot while playing a video game in a first floor apartment in his neighborhood of South Providence, the bullets coming through the ceiling from the apartment above. He didn't know who shot him, and said he's never been in a gang or been in a dispute with anyone. One bullet pierced his lung and just missed his liver. The second bullet cut his forearm. The third went through his right shoulder and came out his back. He was in Rhode Island Hospital for four days.

He had just graduated from a one-year course at a technical school in Massachusetts. He still wants to one day be an electrician.